THE YALE SHAKESPEARE

EDITED BY

Wilbur L. Cross   Tucker Brooke

Published under the Direction
of the
Department of English, Yale University,
on the Fund
Given to the Yale University Press in 1917
by the Members of the
Kingsley Trust Association
(Scroll and Key Society of Yale College)
To Commemorate the Seventy-Fifth Anniversary
of the Founding of the Society.

Enter Tamora pleadinge for her sonnes
going to execution

Tam: Stay Romaine brethren gratious Conquerours
Victorious Titus rue the teares I shed
A mothers teares in passion for her sonne
And if thy sonnes were euer deare to thee
Oh thinke my sonnes to be as deare to mee
Sufficeth not that wee are brought to Roome
To beautify thy triumphes and returne
Captiue to thee and to thy Romaine yoake
But must my sonnes be slaughtered in the streetes
For valiant doinges in theire Countryes cause
Oh if to fighte for kinge and Common weale
Were piety in thine it is in these
Andronicus staine not thy tombe with blood
Wilt thou drawe neere the nature of the Gods
Drawe neere them then in beinge mercifull
Sweete mercy is nobilityes true badge
Thrise noble Titus spare my first borne sonne

Titus: Patient your self madame for by hir that bore me

Aron: And now I curse the day, and yet I thinke
Few come within the compasse of my curse,
Wherein I did not some notorious ill,
As kill a man, or els deuise his deathe,
Rauishe a maid, or plot the way to do it,
Accuse some innocent and forsweare my selfe,
Set deadly enmity betweene two freindes,
Make poore mens cattell breake theire neckes,
Set fire on barnes and haystackes in the nighte,
And bid the owners quenche them with theire teares,
Oft haue I digd vp dead men from theire graues,
And set them vpright at theire deere freindes doore,
Euen almost when theire sorrowes was forgott,
And on theire skinnes, as on the barke of trees,
Haue with my knife carued in Romaine letters,
Let not your sorrow die though I am dead,
Tut I haue done a thousand dreadfull thinges
As willingly as one would kill a fly,
And nothing greeues me hartely indeede
Tamora But that I cannot do ten thousand more &c

·: The Yale Shakespeare :·

THE TRAGEDY OF TITUS ANDRONICUS

EDITED BY

A. M. WITHERSPOON

NEW HAVEN · YALE UNIVERSITY PRESS
LONDON · HUMPHREY MILFORD
OXFORD UNIVERSITY PRESS · MCMXXVI

TABLE OF CONTENTS

The facsimile opposite reproduces, by permission of the owner, the Marquis of Bath, a sheet lately discovered at Longleat by Sir E. K. Chambers and discussed by him as 'The First Illustration to "Shakespeare" ' in 'The Library,' March, 1925. The document, consisting of the single page here photographed, was produced by Henry Peacham, painter and author, in 1595. The sketch at the top shows Tamora and her two kneeling sons appealing to Titus Andronicus for the life of Alarbus, while Aaron the Moor stands at the extreme right.

See Appendix E, page 140.

[DRAMATIS PERSONÆ

SATURNINUS, *Son to the late Emperor of Rome, and afterwards declared Emperor*

BASSIANUS, *Brother to Saturninus, in love with Lavinia*

TITUS ANDRONICUS, *a Roman, General against the Goths*

MARCUS ANDRONICUS, *Tribune of the People, and Brother to Titus*

LUCIUS,
QUINTUS, } *Sons to Titus Andronicus*
MARTIUS,
MUTIUS,

YOUNG LUCIUS, *a Boy, Son to Lucius*

PUBLIUS, *Son to Marcus Andronicus*

SEMPRONIUS,
CAIUS, } *Kinsmen to Titus*
VALENTINE,

ÆMILIUS, *a noble Roman*

ALARBUS,
DEMETRIUS, } *Sons to Tamora*
CHIRON,

AARON, *a Moor, beloved by Tamora*

A Clown

TAMORA, *Queen of the Goths*

LAVINIA, *Daughter to Titus Andronicus*

A Nurse, and a black Child

Senators, Tribunes, Officers, Soldiers, and Attendants

SCENE: *Rome, and the Country near it.*]

Dramatis Personæ; *cf. n.*

The Lamentable Tragedy of
Titus Andronicus

ACT FIRST

Scene One

[*Rome. Before the Capitol. The Tomb of the Andronici appearing*]

*Flourish. Enter the Tribunes and Senators aloft;
and then enter Saturninus and his Followers at
one door, and Bassianus and his Followers at the
other, with drum and colours.*

Sat. Noble patricians, patrons of my right,
Defend the justice of my cause with arms;
And, countrymen, my loving followers,
Plead my successive title with your swords: 4
I am his first-born son that was the last
That wore the imperial diadem of Rome;
Then let my father's honours live in me,
Nor wrong mine age with this indignity.   8
   Bas. Romans, friends, followers, favourers of my
     right,
If ever Bassianus, Cæsar's son,
Were gracious in the eyes of royal Rome,
Keep then this passage to the Capitol,   12
And suffer not dishonour to approach
The imperial seat, to virtue consecrate,
To justice, continence, and nobility;

Scene One, S. d. *aloft; cf. n.*
4 successive title: *title to the succession*
8 age: *seniority*   9 Romans; *cf. n.*

But let desert in pure election shine,   16
And, Romans, fight for freedom in your choice.

Enter Marcus Andronicus, aloft, with the crown.

Mar. Princes, that strive by factions and by friends
Ambitiously for rule and empery,
Know that the people of Rome, for whom we stand 20
A special party, have, by common voice,
In election for the Roman empery,
Chosen Andronicus, surnamed Pius,
For many good and great deserts to Rome;   24
A nobler man, a braver warrior,
Lives not this day within the city walls;
He by the senate is accited home
From weary wars against the barbarous Goths;   28
That, with his sons, a terror to our foes,
Hath yok'd a nation, strong, train'd up in arms.
Ten years are spent since first he undertook
This cause of Rome, and chastised with arms   32
Our enemies' pride: five times he hath return'd
Bleeding to Rome, bearing his valiant sons
In coffins from the field;
And now at last, laden with honour's spoils,   36
Returns the good Andronicus to Rome,
Renowned Titus, flourishing in arms.
Let us entreat, by honour of his name,
Whom worthily you would have now succeed,   40
And in the Capitol and senate's right,
Whom you pretend to honour and adore,
That you withdraw you and abate your strength;
Dismiss your followers, and, as suitors should,   44

16 pure election: *free choice*   19 empery: *imperial power*
22 election: *nomination*   27 accited: *summoned*
35 In coffins from the field; *cf. n.*   42 pretend: *profess*

Plead your deserts in peace and humbleness.

   Sat. How fair the tribune speaks to calm my
     thoughts!

   Bas. Marcus Andronicus, so I do affy
In thy uprightness and integrity,   48
And so I love and honour thee and thine,
Thy noble brother Titus and his sons,
And her to whom my thoughts are humbled all,
Gracious Lavinia, Rome's rich ornament,   52
That I will here dismiss my loving friends,
And to my fortunes and the people's favour
Commit my cause in balance to be weigh'd.

                Exeunt Soldiers [of Bassianus].

   Sat. Friends, that have been thus forward in my
     right,   56
I thank you all and here dismiss you all;
And to the love and favour of my country
Commit myself, my person, and the cause.

              [Exeunt Soldiers of Saturninus.]

Rome, be as just and gracious unto me   60
As I am confident and kind to thee.
Open the gates, and let me in.

   Bas. Tribunes, and me, a poor competitor.

     Flourish. They go up into the Senate-house.

             Enter a Captain.

   Cap. Romans, make way! the good Andronicus,   64
Patron of virtue, Rome's best champion,
Successful in the battles that he fights,
With honour and with fortune is return'd
From where he circumscribed with his sword,   68
And brought to yoke, the enemies of Rome.

47 affy: *have faith*   64 *Cf. n.*
68 circumscribed: *restrained*

*Sound drums and trumpets, and then enter two of
Titus's Sons [Martius and Mutius]; after them
two Men bearing a Coffin covered with black;
then two other Sons [Lucius and Quintus]. After
them, Titus Andronicus; and then Tamora, the
Queen of Goths, and her three Sons, [Alarbus,]
Chiron, and Demetrius, with Aaron the Moor, and
Others, [Prisoners,] as many as can be. They
set down the Coffin, and Titus speaks.*

Tit. Hail, Rome, victorious in thy mourning weeds!
Lo! as the bark, that hath discharg'd her fraught,
Returns with precious lading to the bay   72
From whence at first she weigh'd her anchorage,
Cometh Andronicus, bound with laurel boughs,
To re-salute his country with his tears,
Tears of true joy for his return to Rome.   76
Thou great defender of this Capitol,
Stand gracious to the rites that we intend!
Romans, of five-and-twenty valiant sons,
Half of the number that King Priam had,   80
Behold the poor remains, alive, and dead!
These that survive, let Rome reward with love;
These that I bring unto their latest home,
With burial among their ancestors.   84
Here Goths have given me leave to sheathe my sword.
Titus, unkind and careless of thine own,
Why suffer'st thou thy sons, unburied yet,
To hover on the dreadful shore of Styx?   88
Make way to lay them by their brethren.
                                         They open the tomb.
There greet in silence, as the dead are wont,
And sleep in peace, slain in your country's wars!

70 weeds: *garments*   71 fraught: *freight*
73 anchorage: *anchor*
77 great defender: *Jupiter Capitolinus, to whom the Capitol was sacred*

O sacred receptacle of my joys,   92
Sweet cell of virtue and nobility,
How many sons of mine hast thou in store,
That thou wilt never render to me more!

Luc. Give us the proudest prisoner of the Goths,   96
That we may hew his limbs, and on a pile
Ad manes fratrum sacrifice his flesh,
Before this earthy prison of their bones;
That so the shadows be not unappeas'd,   100
Nor we disturb'd with prodigies on earth.

Tit. I give him you, the noblest that survives,
The eldest son of this distressed queen.

    Tam. Stay, Roman brethren! Gracious con-
            queror,   104
Victorious Titus, rue the tears I shed,
A mother's tears in passion for her son:
And if thy sons were ever dear to thee,
O! think my sons to be as dear to me.   108
Sufficeth not that we are brought to Rome,
To beautify thy triumphs and return,
Captive to thee and to thy Roman yoke,
But must my sons be slaughter'd in the streets,   112
For valiant doings in their country's cause?
O! if to fight for king and commonweal
Were piety in thine, it is in these.
Andronicus, stain not thy tomb with blood!   116
Wilt thou draw near the nature of the gods?
Draw near them then in being merciful;
Sweet mercy is nobility's true badge:
Thrice-noble Titus, spare my first-born son!   120

    Tit. Patient yourself, madam, and pardon me.
These are their brethren, whom your Goths beheld

98 Ad manes fratrum: *to the shades of* [*our*] *brothers; cf. n.*
106 passion: *suffering*   117-119 *Cf. n.*   121 Patient: *quiet*

Alive and dead, and for their brethren slain
Religiously they ask a sacrifice: 124
To this your son is mark'd, and die he must,
T'appease their groaning shadows that are gone.

Luc. Away with him! and make a fire straight;
And with our swords, upon a pile of wood,   128
Let's hew his limbs till they be clean consum'd.

               Exeunt [Titus's] Sons with Alarbus.

Tam. O cruel, irreligious piety!

Chi. Was ever Scythia half so barbarous?

Dem. Oppose not Scythia to ambitious Rome.   132
Alarbus goes to rest, and we survive
To tremble under Titus' threatening look.
Then, madam, stand resolv'd; but hope withal
The self-same gods, that arm'd the Queen of Troy 136
With opportunity of sharp revenge
Upon the Thracian tyrant in his tent,
May favour Tamora, the Queen of Goths—
When Goths were Goths, and Tamora was queen— 140
To quit the bloody wrongs upon her foes.

       Enter the Sons of Andronicus again.

Luc. See, lord and father, how we have perform'd
Our Roman rites. Alarbus' limbs are lopp'd,
And entrails feed the sacrificing fire,   144
Whose smoke, like incense, doth perfume the sky.
Remaineth nought but to inter our brethren,
And with loud 'larums welcome them to Rome.

Tit. Let it be so; and let Andronicus   148
Make this his latest farewell to their souls.

           *Flourish. Then sound trumpets, and lay
                 the coffin in the tomb.*

131 Scythia; *cf. n.*   132 Oppose: *compare*
136 Queen of Troy: *Hecuba*   138 Thracian tyrant; *cf. n.*
141 quit: *requite*

In peace and honour rest you here, my sons;
Rome's readiest champions, repose you here in rest,
Secure from worldly chances and mishaps!   152
Here lurks no treason, here no envy swells,
Here grow no damned grudges, here are no storms,
No noise, but silence and eternal sleep:
In peace and honour rest you here, my sons!   156

Enter Lavinia.

Lav. In peace and honour live Lord Titus long;
My noble lord and father, live in fame!
Lo! at this tomb my tributary tears
I render for my brethren's obsequies;   160
And at thy feet I kneel, with tears of joy
Shed on the earth for thy return to Rome.
O! bless me here with thy victorious hand,
Whose fortunes Rome's best citizens applaud.   164

Tit. Kind Rome, that hast thus lovingly reserv'd
The cordial of mine age to glad my heart!
Lavinia, live; outlive thy father's days,
And fame's eternal date, for virtue's praise!   168

[*Enter, below, Marcus Andronicus and Tribunes; re-
enter Saturninus, Bassianus, and Others.*]

Mar. Long live Lord Titus, my beloved brother,
Gracious triumpher in the eyes of Rome!

Tit. Thanks, gentle Tribune, noble brother Marcus.

Mar. And welcome, nephews, from successful
wars,   172
You that survive, and you that sleep in fame!
Fair lords, your fortunes are alike in all,
That in your country's service drew your swords;
But safer triumph is this funeral pomp,   176

154 grudges; *cf. n.*   165 reserv'd: *preserved*
168 date: *duration; cf. n.*

That hath aspir'd to Solon's happiness,
And triumphs over chance in honour's bed.
Titus Andronicus, the people of Rome,
Whose friend in justice thou hast ever been,   180
Send thee by me, their tribune and their trust,
This palliament of white and spotless hue;
And name thee in election for the empire,
With these our late-deceased emperor's sons: 184
Be *candidatus* then, and put it on,
And help to set a head on headless Rome.

   Tit. A better head her glorious body fits
Than his that shakes for age and feebleness.   188
What should I don this robe, and trouble you?
Be chosen with proclamations to-day,
To-morrow yield up rule, resign my life,
And set abroad new business for you all?   192
Rome, I have been thy soldier forty years,
And led my country's strength successfully,
And buried one-and-twenty valiant sons,
Knighted in field, slain manfully in arms,   196
In right and service of their noble country.
Give me a staff of honour for mine age,
But not a sceptre to control the world:
Upright he held it, lords, that held it last.   200

   Mar. Titus, thou shalt obtain and ask the empery.

   Sat. Proud and ambitious tribune, canst thou tell?—

   Tit. Patience, Prince Saturninus.

   Sat.   Romans, do me right:
Patricians, draw your swords, and sheathe them
     not   204
Till Saturninus be Rome's emperor.

177 Solon's happiness; *cf. n.*
182 palliament: *cloak* (Lat. *pallium*), *Roman robe of state*
183 name thee in election: *nominate thee*
185 candidatus: *a candidate*   189 What: *why*
201 obtain and ask: *obtain by merely asking*

Andronicus, would thou wert shipp'd to hell,
Rather than rob me of the people's hearts!

   Luc. Proud Saturnine, interrupter of the good   208
That noble-minded Titus means to thee!

   Tit. Content thee, prince; I will restore to thee
The people's hearts, and wean them from themselves.

   Bas. Andronicus, I do not flatter thee,   212
But honour thee, and will do till I die;
My faction if thou strengthen with thy friends,
I will most thankful be; and thanks to men
Of noble minds is honourable meed.   216

   Tit. People of Rome, and people's tribunes here,
I ask your voices and your suffrages:
Will you bestow them friendly on Andronicus?

   Tribunes. To gratify the good Andronicus,   220
And gratulate his safe return to Rome,
The people will accept whom he admits.

   Tit. Tribunes, I thank you; and this suit I make,
That you create your emperor's eldest son,   224
Lord Saturnine; whose virtues will, I hope,
Reflect on Rome as Titan's rays on earth,
And ripen justice in this commonweal:
Then, if you will elect by my advice,   228
Crown him, and say, 'Long live our emperor!'

   Mar. With voices and applause of every sort,
Patricians and plebeians, we create
Lord Saturninus Rome's great emperor,   232
And say, 'Long live our Emperor Saturnine!'
                A long flourish till they come down.

   Sat. Titus Andronicus, for thy favours done
To us in our election this day,
I give thee thanks in part of thy deserts,   236

217 people's tribunes; *cf. n.*   221 gratulate: *celebrate*
224 create: *elect*   226 Titan's: *the sun god's*

And will with deeds requite thy gentleness:
And, for an onset, Titus, to advance
Thy name and honourable family,
Lavinia will I make my empress,   240
Rome's royal mistress, mistress of my heart,
And in the sacred Pantheon her espouse.
Tell me, Andronicus, doth this motion please thee?

   Tit. It doth, my worthy lord; and in this match 244
I hold me highly honour'd of your Grace:
And here in sight of Rome to Saturnine,
King and commander of our commonweal,
The wide world's emperor, do I consecrate   248
My sword, my chariot, and my prisoners;
Presents well worthy Rome's imperious lord:
Receive them then, the tribute that I owe,
Mine honour's ensigns humbled at thy feet.   252

   Sat. Thanks, noble Titus, father of my life!
How proud I am of thee and of thy gifts
Rome shall record, and, when I do forget
The least of these unspeakable deserts,   256
Romans, forget your fealty to me.

   Tit. [*To Tamora.*] Now, madam, are you prisoner
    to an emperor;
To him that, for your honour and your state,
Will use you nobly and your followers.   260

   Sat. [*Aside.*] A goodly lady, trust me; of the hue
That I would choose, were I to choose anew.
[*To Tamora.*] Clear up, fair queen, that cloudy
    countenance:
Though chance of war hath wrought this change of
    cheer,   264
Thou com'st not to be made a scorn in Rome:

237 gentleness: *noble conduct*   238 onset: *beginning*
264 cheer: *countenance*

Princely shall be thy usage every way.
Rest on my word, and let not discontent
Daunt all your hopes: madam, he comforts you   268
Can make you greater than the Queen of Goths.
Lavinia, you are not displeas'd with this?

    Lav. Not I, my lord; sith true nobility
Warrants these words in princely courtesy.   272

    Sat. Thanks, sweet Lavinia.   Romans, let us go;
Ransomless here we set our prisoners free:
Proclaim our honours, lords, with trump and drum.
          [*Flourish.   Saturninus courts Tamora
                    in dumb show.*]

    Bas. [*Seizing Lavinia.*] Lord Titus, by your leave,
    this maid is mine.   276

    Tit. How, sir! Are you in earnest then, my lord?

    Bas. Ay, noble Titus; and resolv'd withal
To do myself this reason and this right.

    Mar. Suum cuique is our Roman justice: 280
This prince in justice seizeth but his own.

    Luc. And that he will, and shall, if Lucius live.

    Tit. Traitors, avaunt!   Where is the emperor's
    guard?
Treason, my lord! Lavinia is surpris'd.   284

    Sat. Surpris'd! By whom?

    Bas.   By him that justly may
Bear his betroth'd from all the world away.
              [*Exeunt Marcus and Bassianus
                  with Lavinia.*]

    Mut. Brothers, help to convey her hence away,
And with my sword I'll keep this door safe.   288
            [*Exeunt Lucius, Quintus, and Martius.*]

    Tit. Follow, my lord, and I'll soon bring her back.

269 Can: *who can*   271 sith: *since*
280 Suum cuique: *to every man his due*

Mut. My lord, you pass not here.

Tit.   What! villain boy;
Barr'st me my way in Rome?   *He kills him.*

Mut.   Help, Lucius, help!

[*Exeunt, during the fray, Saturninus, Tamora, Demetrius, Chiron, and Aaron. Re-enter Lucius.*]

Luc. My lord, you are unjust; and, more than so, 292
In wrongful quarrel you have slain your son.

Tit. Nor thou, nor he, are any sons of mine;
My sons would never so dishonour me.
Traitor, restore Lavinia to the emperor.   296

Luc. Dead, if you will; but not to be his wife
That is another's lawful promis'd love.   [*Exit.*]

*Enter, aloft, the Emperor with Tamora and her two
            Sons, and Aaron the Moor.*

Sat. No, Titus, no; the emperor needs her not,
Nor her, nor thee, nor any of thy stock: 300
I'll trust, by leisure, him that mocks me once;
Thee never, nor thy traitorous haughty sons,
Confederates all thus to dishonour me.
Was none in Rome to make a stale   304
But Saturnine? Full well, Andronicus,
Agreed these deeds with that proud brag of thine,
That saidst I begg'd the empire at thy hands.

Tit. O monstrous! what reproachful words are
      these!   308

Sat. But go thy ways; go, give that changing piece
To him that flourish'd for her with his sword.
A valiant son-in-law thou shalt enjoy;
One fit to bandy with thy lawless sons,   312

301 I'll . . . leisure: *I'll be in no hurry to trust*
304 stale: *laughing-stock*   309 piece: *wench*
312 bandy: *contend; cf. n.*

To ruffle in the commonwealth of Rome.

 Tit. These words are razors to my wounded heart.

 Sat. And therefore, lovely Tamora, Queen of Goths,
That like the stately Phœbe 'mongst her nymphs, 316
Dost overshine the gallant'st dames of Rome,
If thou be pleas'd with this my sudden choice,
Behold, I choose thee, Tamora, for my bride,
And will create thee Empress of Rome. 320
Speak, Queen of Goths, dost thou applaud my choice?
And here I swear by all the Roman gods,
Sith priest and holy water are so near,
And tapers burn so bright, and everything 324
In readiness for Hymenæus stand,
I will not re-salute the streets of Rome,
Or climb my palace, till from forth this place
I lead espous'd my bride along with me. 328

 Tam. And here, in sight of heaven, to Rome I swear,
If Saturnine advance the Queen of Goths,
She will a handmaid be to his desires,
A loving nurse, a mother to his youth. 332

 Sat. Ascend, fair queen, Pantheon. Lords, accompany
Your noble emperor, and his lovely bride,
Sent by the heavens for Prince Saturnine,
Whose wisdom hath her fortune conquered: 336
There shall we consummate our spousal rights.

       Exeunt omnes [*but Titus*].

 Tit. I am not bid to wait upon this bride.
Titus, when wert thou wont to walk alone,
Dishonour'd thus, and challenged of wrongs? 340

   Enter Marcus and Titus's Sons.

313 ruffle: *be disorderly*   323 priest and holy water; *cf. n.*
325 Hymenæus: *Hymen, the god of marriage*
338 bid: *invited*   340 challenged: *accused*

Mar. O Titus, see! O, see what thou hast done!
In a bad quarrel slain a virtuous son.

Tit. No, foolish tribune, no; no son of mine,
Nor thou, nor these, confederates in the deed   344
That hath dishonour'd all our family:
Unworthy brother, and unworthy sons!

Luc. But let us give him burial, as becomes;
Give Mutius burial with our brethren.   348

Tit. Traitors, away! he rests not in this tomb.
This monument five hundred years hath stood,
Which I have sumptuously re-edified:
Here none but soldiers and Rome's servitors   352
Repose in fame; none basely slain in brawls.
Bury him where you can; he comes not here.

Mar. My lord, this is impiety in you.
My nephew Mutius' deeds do plead for him;   356
He must be buried with his brethren.

                              Titus's two Sons speak.

[*Quin.*] ⎫
[*Mart.*] ⎬ And shall, or him we will accompany.

Tit. And shall!   What villain was it spake that
    word?

                    Titus's Son [*Quintus*] *speaks.*

[*Quin.*] He that would vouch it in any place but
    here.   360

Tit. What! would you bury him in my despite?

Mar. No, noble Titus; but entreat of thee
To pardon Mutius, and to bury him.

Tit. Marcus, even thou hast struck upon my
    crest,   364
And, with these boys, mine honour thou hast wounded:
My foes I do repute you every one;
So trouble me no more, but get you gone.

351 re-edified: *restored*

1. Son [Mart.] He is not with himself; let us withdraw.   368
2. Son [Quin.] Not I, till Mutius' bones be buried.
                    The Brother and the Sons kneel.
Mar. Brother, for in that name doth nature plead,—
2. Son. Father, and in that name doth nature
  speak,—
Tit. Speak thou no more, if all the rest will
  speed.   372
Mar. Renowned Titus, more than half my soul,—
Luc. Dear father, soul and substance of us all,—
Mar. Suffer thy brother Marcus to inter
His noble nephew here in virtue's nest,   376
That died in honour and Lavinia's cause.
Thou art a Roman; be not barbarous:
The Greeks upon advice did bury Ajax
That slew himself; and wise Laertes' son   380
Did graciously plead for his funerals.
Let not young Mutius, then, that was thy joy,
Be barr'd his entrance here.
  Tit.   Rise, Marcus, rise.
The dismal'st day is this that e'er I saw,   384
To be dishonour'd by my sons in Rome!
Well, bury him, and bury me the next.
                        They put him in the tomb.
Luc. There lie thy bones, sweet Mutius, with thy
  friends,
Till we with trophies do adorn thy tomb.   388
                        They all kneel and say,
[All.] No man shed tears for noble Mutius;
He lives in fame that died in virtue's cause.
              [Exeunt all but Marcus and Titus.]

---

368 not with himself: *beside himself*   372 will speed: *wish to succeed*
379 upon advice: *after deliberation*   Ajax; *cf. n.*
380 Laertes' son: *Ulysses*   381 funerals: *obsequies*

Mar. My lord,—to step out of these dreary
 dumps,—

How comes it that the subtle Queen of Goths 392
Is of a sudden thus advanc'd in Rome?

 Tit. I know not, Marcus; but I know it is;
Whether by device or no, the heavens can tell.
Is she not, then, beholding to the man 396
That brought her for this high good turn so far?

 [*Mar.*] Yes, and will nobly him remunerate.

*Flourish. Enter the Emperor, Tamora and her two
  Sons, with the Moor, at one door. Enter, at the
  other door, Bassianus and Lavinia, with Others.*

 Sat. So, Bassianus, you have play'd your prize:
God give you joy, sir, of your gallant bride. 400

 Bas. And you of yours, my lord! I say no more,
Nor wish no less; and so I take my leave.

 Sat. Traitor, if Rome have law or we have power,
Thou and thy faction shall repent this rape. 404

 Bas. Rape call you it, my lord, to seize my own,
My true-betrothed love and now my wife?
But let the laws of Rome determine all;
Meanwhile, I am possess'd of that is mine. 408

 Sat. 'Tis good, sir: you are very short with us;
But, if we live, we'll be as sharp with you.

 Bas. My lord, what I have done, as best I may,
Answer I must and shall do with my life. 412
Only thus much I give your Grace to know:
By all the duties that I owe to Rome,
This noble gentleman, Lord Titus here,
Is in opinion and in honour wrong'd; 416
That, in the rescue of Lavinia,

---

391 dumps: *low spirits*   395 device: *scheming*
396 beholding: *beholden*   399 play'd your prize; *cf. n.*
416 opinion: *reputation*

With his own hand did slay his youngest son,
In zeal to you and highly mov'd to wrath
To be controll'd in that he frankly gave: 420
Receive him, then, to favour, Saturnine,
That hath express'd himself in all his deeds
A father and a friend to thee and Rome.

Tit. Prince Bassianus, leave to plead my deeds: 424
'Tis thou and those that have dishonour'd me.
Rome and the righteous heavens be my judge,
How I have lov'd and honour'd Saturnine!

Tam. My worthy lord, if ever Tamora   428
Were gracious in those princely eyes of thine,
Then hear me speak indifferently for all;
And at my suit, sweet, pardon what is past.

Sat. What, madam! be dishonour'd openly,   432
And basely put it up without revenge?

Tam. Not so, my lord; the gods of Rome forfend
I should be author to dishonour you!
But on mine honour dare I undertake   436
For good Lord Titus' innocence in all,
Whose fury not dissembled speaks his griefs.
Then, at my suit, look graciously on him;
Lose not so noble a friend on vain suppose,   440
Nor with sour looks afflict his gentle heart.
[*Aside to Saturninus.*] My lord, be rul'd by me, be
    won at last;
Dissemble all your griefs and discontents:
You are but newly planted in your throne;   444
Lest, then, the people, and patricians too,
Upon a just survey, take Titus' part,
And so supplant you for ingratitude,

420 controll'd: *restrained, hindered*   frankly: *freely*
424 leave: *cease*   430 indifferently: *impartially*
433 put it up: *put up with it*   434 forfend: *forbid*
435 author . . . you: *author of your dishonor*
436 undertake: *vouch*   440 suppose: *supposition*

Which Rome reputes to be a heinous sin,   448
Yield at entreats, and then let me alone.
I'll find a day to massacre them all,
And raze their faction and their family,
The cruel father, and his traitorous sons,   452
To whom I sued for my dear son's life;
And make them know what 'tis to let a queen
Kneel in the streets and beg for grace in vain.
[*Aloud.*] Come, come, sweet emperor—come, Androni-
    cus—   456
Take up this good old man, and cheer the heart
That dies in tempest of thy angry frown.

    Sat. Rise, Titus, rise; my empress hath prevail'd.

    Tit. I thank your majesty, and her, my lord.   460
These words, these looks, infuse new life in me.

    Tam. Titus, I am incorporate in Rome,
A Roman now adopted happily,
And must advise the emperor for his good.   464
This day all quarrels die, Andronicus;
And let it be mine honour, good my lord,
That I have reconcil'd your friends and you.
For you, Prince Bassianus, I have pass'd   468
My word and promise to the emperor,
That you will be more mild and tractable.
And fear not, lords, and you, Lavinia:
By my advice, all humbled on your knees,   472
You shall ask pardon of his majesty.

    [*Marcus, Lavinia, and the Sons of Titus kneel.*]

    Luc. We do; and vow to heaven and to his highness,
That what we did was mildly as we might,
Tend'ring our sister's honour and our own.   476

---

449 at entreats: *to entreaties*   let me alone: *leave everything to me*
462 incorporate: *incorporated, established*
475 mildly as we might: *as gently as possible*
476 Tend'ring: *having a tender regard for*

Mar. That, on mine honour, here I do protest.

Sat. Away, and talk not; trouble us no more.

Tam. Nay, nay, sweet emperor, we must all be
    friends:

The tribune and his nephews kneel for grace;   480

I will not be denied: sweetheart, look back.

Sat. Marcus, for thy sake, and thy brother's here,

And at my lovely Tamora's entreats,

I do remit these young men's heinous faults: 484

Stand up.

        [Marcus, Lavinia, and the Others rise.]

Lavinia, though you left me like a churl,

I found a friend, and sure as death I sware

I would not part a bachelor from the priest.   488

Come; if the emperor's court can feast two brides,

You are my guest, Lavinia, and your friends.

This day shall be a love-day, Tamora.

Tit. To-morrow, an it please your majesty   492

To hunt the panther and the hart with me,

With horn and hound we'll give your Grace *bon jour*.

Sat. Be it so, Titus, and gramercy too.

                          Exeunt.

ACT SECOND

Scene One

[Rome.   Before the Palace]

Flourish.   Enter Aaron alone.

Aar. Now climbeth Tamora Olympus' top,

Safe out of Fortune's shot; and sits aloft,

485 Stand up; *cf. n.*   486 churl: *a mean, worthless person*
488 part: *depart*   491 love-day; *cf. n.*
493 To hunt the panther; *cf. n.*   494 bon jour: *good morning*
495 gramercy: *many thanks (Fr. grand merci)*

Secure of thunder's crack or lightning flash,
Advanc'd above pale envy's threat'ning reach.   4
As when the golden sun salutes the morn,
And, having gilt the ocean with his beams,
Gallops the zodiac in his glistering coach,
And overlooks the highest-peering hills;   8
So Tamora.
Upon her wit doth earthly honour wait
And virtue stoops and trembles at her frown.
Then, Aaron, arm thy heart, and fit thy thoughts   12
To mount aloft with thy imperial mistress,
And mount her pitch, whom thou in triumph long
Hast prisoner held, fetter'd in amorous chains,
And faster bound to Aaron's charming eyes   16
Than is Prometheus tied to Caucasus.
Away with slavish weeds and servile thoughts!
I will be bright, and shine in pearl and gold,
To wait upon this new-made empress.   20
To wait, said I? to wanton with this queen,
This goddess, this Semiramis, this nymph,
This siren, that will charm Rome's Saturnine,
And see his shipwrack and his commonweal's.   24
Hollo! what storm is this?

Enter Chiron and Demetrius, braving.

Dem. Chiron, thy years want wit, thy wit wants
    edge
And manners, to intrude where I am grac'd,
And may, for aught thou know'st, affected be.   28
    Chi. Demetrius, thou dost overween in all

---

3 Secure of: *safe from*   7 Gallops: *gallops over*
8 overlooks: *looks down on*   14 pitch; *cf. n.*
16 charming: *having power to charm, or cast a spell*
17 Prometheus; *cf. n.*   18 weeds: *garments*
22 Semiramis; *cf. n.*   25 S. d. braving: *defying each other*
27 grac'd: *favored*   28 affected: *loved*
29 dost overween: *art presumptuous*

And so in this, to bear me down with braves.
'Tis not the difference of a year or two
Makes me less gracious or thee more fortunate:　32
I am as able and as fit as thou
To serve, and to deserve, my mistress' grace;
And that my sword upon thee shall approve,
And plead my passions for Lavinia's love.　36

　　Aar. Clubs, clubs! these lovers will not keep the
　　　peace.

　　Dem. Why, boy, although our mother, unadvis'd,
Gave you a dancing-rapier by your side,
Are you so desperate grown, to threat your friends?　40
Go to; have your lath glu'd within your sheath
Till you know better how to handle it.

　　Chi. Meanwhile, sir, with the little skill I have,
Full well shalt thou perceive how much I dare.　44

　　Dem. Ay, boy, grow ye so brave?　　*They draw.*

　　Aar.　　　　　　　Why, how now, lords!
So near the emperor's palace dare you draw,
And maintain such a quarrel openly?
Full well I wot the ground of all this grudge:　48
I would not for a million of gold
The cause were known to them it most concerns;
Nor would your noble mother for much more
Be so dishonour'd in the court of Rome.　52
For shame, put up.

　　Dem.　　　　　Not I, till I have sheath'd
My rapier in his bosom, and withal
Thrust those reproachful speeches down his throat
That he hath breath'd in my dishonour here.　56

　　Chi. For that I am prepar'd and full resolv'd,

---

30 braves: *brags*　　　　　　　　　　35 approve: *prove*
37 Clubs, clubs!: *cf. n.*　　　38 unadvis'd: *thoughtlessly, rashly*
39 dancing-rapier: *a sword worn only for ornament*
41 lath: *contemptuous term for sword; cf. n.*　　　48 wot: *know*
53 put up: *sheathe your swords*　　　Not I; *cf. n.*

Foul-spoken coward, that thunder'st with thy tongue,
And with thy weapon nothing dar'st perform!

   Aar. Away, I say!   60
Now, by the gods that warlike Goths adore,
This petty brabble will undo us all.
Why, lords, and think you not how dangerous
It is to jet upon a prince's right?   64
What! is Lavinia then become so loose,
Or Bassianus so degenerate,
That for her love such quarrels may be broach'd
Without controlment, justice, or revenge?   68
Young lords, beware! an should the empress know
This discord's ground, the music would not please.

   Chi. I care not, I, knew she and all the world:
I love Lavinia more than all the world.   72

   Dem. Youngling, learn thou to make some **meaner**
     choice:
Lavinia is thine elder brother's hope.

   Aar. Why, are ye mad? or know ye not in Rome
How furious and impatient they be,   76
And cannot brook competitors in love?
I tell you, lords, you do but plot your deaths
By this device.

   Chi.   Aaron, a thousand deaths
Would I propose, to achieve her whom I love.   80

   Aar. To achieve her! how?

   Dem.   Why mak'st thou it so strange?
She is a woman, therefore may be woo'd;
She is a woman, therefore may be won;
She is Lavinia, therefore must be lov'd.   84
What, man! more water glideth by the mill
Than wots the miller of; and easy it is

---

62 brabble: *squabble, brawl*   64 jet: *encroach*
70 ground; *cf. n.*   80 propose: *risk, undertake*   achieve: *win*
82 She is a woman; *cf. n.*   85 water glideth by the mill; *cf. n.*

Of a cut loaf to steal a shive, we know:

Though Bassianus be the emperor's brother,   88

Better than he have worn Vulcan's badge.

    Aar. [*Aside.*] Ay, and as good as Saturninus may.

    Dem. Then why should he despair that knows to
        court it

With words, fair looks, and liberality?   92

What! hast thou not full often struck a doe,

And borne her cleanly by the keeper's nose?

    Aar. Why, then, it seems, some certain snatch or so

Would serve your turns.

    Chi.   Ay, so the turn were serv'd. 96

    Dem. Aaron, thou hast hit it.

    Aar.   Would you had hit it too!

Then should not we be tir'd with this ado.

Why, hark ye, hark ye! and are you such fools

To square for this? Would it offend you, then,   100

That both should speed?

    Chi.   Faith, not me.

    Dem. Nor me, so I were one.

    Aar. For shame, be friends, and join for that you
        jar:

'Tis policy and stratagem must do   104

That you affect; and so must you resolve

That what you cannot as you would achieve,

You must perforce accomplish as you may.

Take this of me: Lucrece was not more chaste   108

Than this Lavinia, Bassianus' love.

A speedier course than ling'ring languishment

Must we pursue, and I have found the path.

87 shive: *slice*   89 Vulcan's badge; *cf. n.*
100 square: *put oneself in a boxing attitude, quarrel*
103 that you jar: *that which you are quarreling about*
105 affect: *desire*   108 Lucrece; *cf. n.*
110 ling'ring languishment: *a long-drawn-out courtship*

My lords, a solemn hunting is in hand;   112
There will the lovely Roman ladies troop:
The forest walks are wide and spacious,
And many unfrequented plots there are
Fitted by kind for rape and villainy: 116
Single you thither, then, this dainty doe,
And strike her home by force, if not by words:
This way, or not at all, stand you in hope.
Come, come, our empress, with her sacred wit   120
To villainy and vengeance consecrate,
Will we acquaint with all that we intend;
And she shall file our engines with advice,
That will not suffer you to square yourselves,   124
But to your wishes' height advance you both.
The emperor's court is like the house of Fame,
The palace full of tongues, of eyes, and ears:
The woods are ruthless, dreadful, deaf, and dull;   128
There speak, and strike, brave boys, and take your
    turns;
There serve your lusts, shadow'd from heaven's eye,
And revel in Lavinia's treasury.
    Chi. Thy counsel, lad, smells of no cowardice.   132
    Dem. Sit fas aut nefas, till I find the stream
To cool this heat, a charm to calm these fits,
Per Styga, per manes vehor.   *Exeunt.*

112 solemn: *formal, grand*   116 by kind: *by nature*
120 sacred; *cf. n.*
123 file our engines: *sharpen, or finish off, our designs*
124 square yourselves: *settle it between yourselves*
126 house of Fame; *cf. n.*
133 Sit fas aut nefas: *Be it right or wrong*
135 Per Styga, per manes vehor: *I am borne across the Styx, and
among the shades of the dead; cf. n.*

Scene Two

[*A Forest near Rome*]

*Enter Titus Andronicus and his three Sons, making a
    noise with hounds and horns, and Marcus.*

Tit. The hunt is up, the morn is bright and grey,
The fields are fragrant and the woods are green.
Uncouple here and let us make a bay,
And wake the emperor and his lovely bride,   4
And rouse the prince and ring a hunter's peal,
That all the court may echo with the noise.
Sons, let it be your charge, as it is ours,
To attend the emperor's person carefully: 8
I have been troubled in my sleep this night,
But dawning day new comfort hath inspir'd.

                                        Wind horns.

*Here a cry of hounds, and wind horns in a peal, then
    enter Saturninus, Tamora, Bassianus, Lavinia,
    Chiron, Demetrius, and their Attendants.*

Many good morrows to your majesty;
Madam, to you as many and as good;   12
I promised your Grace a hunter's peal.
    Sat. And you have rung it lustily, my lord;
Somewhat too early for new-married ladies.
    Bas. Lavinia, how say you?
    Lav.   I say, no;   16
I have been broad awake two hours and more.
    Sat. Come on, then; horse and chariots let us have,
And to our sport.—[*To Tamora.*] Madam, now shall
    ye see
Our Roman hunting.

1 grey; *cf. n.*   3 Uncouple here; *cf. n.*   bay: *barking*
9 I have been troubled; *cf. n.*

Mar.   I have dogs, my lord,   20
Will rouse the proudest panther in the chase,
And climb the highest promontory top.

Tit. And I have horse will follow where the game
Makes way, and run like swallows o'er the plain.   24

Dem. [*Aside.*] Chiron, we hunt not, we, with horse
    nor hound,
But hope to pluck a dainty doe to ground.   *Exeunt.*

Scene Three

[*A lonely part of the Forest*]

Enter Aaron alone [*with a bag of gold*].

Aar. He that had wit would think that I had none,
To bury so much gold under a tree,
And never after to inherit it.
Let him that thinks of me so abjectly   4
Know that this gold must coin a stratagem,
Which, cunningly effected, will beget
A very excellent piece of villainy:
And so repose, sweet gold, for their unrest   8
That have their alms out of the empress' chest.

[*Hides the gold.*]

Enter Tamora to the Moor.

Tam. My lovely Aaron, wherefore look'st thou sad,
When everything doth make a gleeful boast?
The birds chant melody on every bush,   12
The snake lies rolled in the cheerful sun,
The green leaves quiver with the cooling wind,
And make a chequer'd shadow on the ground.

23 horse: *horses*   24 Makes way: *opens up a passage*
3 inherit: *possess*   9 alms . . . chest; *cf. n.*

Under their sweet shade, Aaron, let us sit, 16
And, whilst the babbling echo mocks the hounds,
Replying shrilly to the well-tun'd horns,
As if a double hunt were heard at once,
Let us sit down and mark their yelping noise; 20
And after conflict, such as was suppos'd
The wandering prince and Dido once enjoy'd,
When with a happy storm they were surpris'd,
And curtain'd with a counsel-keeping cave, 24
We may, each wreathed in the other's arms,
Our pastimes done, possess a golden slumber;
Whiles hounds and horns and sweet melodious birds
Be unto us as is a nurse's song 28
Of lullaby to bring her babe asleep.

Aar. Madam, though Venus govern your desires,
Saturn is dominator over mine:
What signifies my deadly-standing eye, 32
My silence and my cloudy melancholy,
My fleece of woolly hair that now uncurls
Even as an adder when she doth unroll
To do some fatal execution? 36
No, madam, these are no venereal signs:
Vengeance is in my heart, death in my hand,
Blood and revenge are hammering in my head.
Hark, Tamora, the empress of my soul, 40
Which never hopes more heaven than rests in thee:
This is the day of doom for Bassianus;
His Philomel must lose her tongue to-day,
Thy sons make pillage of her chastity, 44
And wash their hands in Bassianus' blood.
Seest thou this letter? take it up, I pray thee,

17 echo mocks the hounds, etc.; *cf. n.*
22 The wandering prince: *Æneas* (*cf. Vergil, Æneid* 4. 165 *ff.*)
23 happy: *lucky*   31 Saturn is dominator; *cf. n.*
32 deadly-standing: *fixedly staring like that of the dead*
37 venereal: *erotic*   43 Philomel; *cf. n.*

And give the king this fatal-plotted scroll.
Now question me no more; we are espied;   48
Here comes a parcel of our hopeful booty,
Which dreads not yet their lives' destruction.

Enter Bassianus and Lavinia.

Tam. Ah! my sweet Moor, sweeter to me than life!

Aar. No more, great empress; Bassianus comes: 52
Be cross with him; and I'll go fetch thy sons
To back thy quarrels, whatsoe'er they be.   [*Exit.*]

Bas. Whom have we here?   Rome's royal empress,
Unfurnish'd of her well-beseeming troop?   56
Or is it Dian, habited like her,
Who hath abandoned her holy groves,
To see the general hunting in this forest?

Tam. Saucy controller of our private steps!   60
Had I the power that some say Dian had,
Thy temples should be planted presently
With horns, as was Actæon's; and the hounds
Should drive upon thy new-transformed limbs,   64
Unmannerly intruder as thou art!

Lav. Under your patience, gentle empress,
'Tis thought you have a goodly gift in horning;
And to be doubted that your Moor and you   68
Are singled forth to try experiments.
Jove shield your husband from his hounds to-day!
'Tis pity they should take him for a stag.

Bas. Believe me, queen, your swarth Cimmerian 72
Doth make your honour of his body's hue,
Spotted, detested, and abominable.
Why are you sequester'd from all your train,
Dismounted from your snow-white goodly steed,   76

49 parcel: *part*
56 well-beseeming troop: *the guard of honor suitable to an empress*
62 presently: *immediately*   63 horns . . . Actæon's; *cf. n.*
64 drive upon: *rush upon*   72 Cimmerian; *cf. n.*

And wander'd hither to an obscure plot,
Accompanied but with a barbarous Moor,
If foul desire had not conducted you?

   Lav. And, being intercepted in your sport,   80
Great reason that my noble lord be rated
For sauciness. I pray you, let us hence,
And let her joy her raven-colour'd love;
This valley fits the purpose passing well.   84

   Bas. The king my brother shall have note of this.

   Lav. Ay, for these slips have made him noted long:
Good king, to be so mightily abus'd!

   Tam. Why have I patience to endure all this?   88

Enter Chiron and Demetrius.

   Dem. How now, dear sovereign, and our gracious
      mother!
Why doth your highness look so pale and wan?

   Tam. Have I not reason, think you, to look pale?
These two have 'tic'd me hither to this place: 92
A barren detested vale, you see, it is;
The trees, though summer, yet forlorn and lean,
O'ercome with moss and baleful mistletoe:
Here never shines the sun; here nothing breeds,   96
Unless the nightly owl or fatal raven:
And when they show'd me this abhorred pit,
They told me, here, at dead time of the night,
A thousand fiends, a thousand hissing snakes,   100
Ten thousand swelling toads, as many urchins,
Would make such fearful and confused cries,
As any mortal body hearing it
Should straight fall mad, or else die suddenly.   104
No sooner had they told this hellish tale,

83 joy: *enjoy*   86 slips: *offences; cf. n.*   87 abus'd: *deceived*
92 'tic'd: *enticed*   93 barren detested vale; *cf. n.*
97 fatal: *evil-omened*   101 urchins: *hedgehogs*

But straight they told me they would bind me here
Unto the body of a dismal yew,
And leave me to this miserable death: 108
And then they call'd me foul adulteress,
Lascivious Goth, and all the bitterest terms
That ever ear did hear to such effect;
And, had you not by wondrous fortune come,   112
This vengeance on me had they executed.
Revenge it, as you love your mother's life,
Or be ye not henceforth call'd my children.

    Dem. This is a witness that I am thy son.   116
                     Stab him [*i.e. Bassianus*].

    Chi. And this for me, struck home to show my
    strength.
             [*Also stabs Bassianus, who dies.*]

    Lav. Ay, come, Semiramis, nay, barbarous Tamora;
For no name fits thy nature but thy own.

    Tam. Give me thy poniard; you shall know, my
    boys,   120
Your mother's hand shall right your mother's wrong.

    Dem. Stay, madam; here is more belongs to her:
First thrash the corn, then after burn the straw.
This minion stood upon her chastity,   124
Upon her nuptial vow, her loyalty,
And with that painted hope braves your mightiness:
And shall she carry this unto her grave?

    Chi. An if she do, I would I were an eunuch.   128
Drag hence her husband to some secret hole,
And make his dead trunk pillow to our lust.

    Tam. But when ye have the honey ye desire,
Let not this wasp outlive, us both to sting.   132

    Chi. I warrant you, madam, we will make that sure.

110 Lascivious Goth; *cf. n.*
124 minion: *saucy person*   stood: *prided herself*
126 painted: *unreal, false* (?)*; cf. n.*

Come, mistress, now perforce we will enjoy
That nice-preserved honesty of yours.

   Lav. O Tamora! thou bear'st a woman's face,— 136

   Tam. I will not hear her speak; away with her!

   Lav. Sweet lords, entreat her hear me but a word.

   Dem. Listen, fair madam: let it be your glory

To see her tears; but be your heart to them   140
As unrelenting flint to drops of rain.

   Lav. When did the tiger's young ones teach the
      dam?

O! do not learn her wrath; she taught it thee;

The milk thou suck'dst from her did turn to
      marble;   144

Even at thy teat thou hadst thy tyranny.

Yet every mother breeds not sons alike:

[*To Chiron.*] Do thou entreat her show a woman pity.

   Chi. What! wouldst thou have me prove myself a
      bastard?   148

   Lav. 'Tis true! the raven doth not hatch a lark:

Yet have I heard—O could I find it now!—

The lion mov'd with pity did endure

To have his princely paws par'd all away.   152

Some say that ravens foster forlorn children,

The whilst their own birds famish in their nests:

O, be to me, though thy hard heart say no,

Nothing so kind, but something pitiful!   156

   Tam. I know not what it means; away with her!

   Lav. O, let me teach thee! for my father's sake,

That gave thee life when well he might have slain
      thee,

Be not obdurate, open thy deaf ears.   160

   Tam. Hadst thou in person ne'er offended me,

---

135 nice-preserved: *prudishly preserved*   143 learn: *teach*
152 paws: *i.e. claws; cf. n.*   153 ravens . . . children; *cf. n.*

Even for his sake am I pitiless.
Remember, boys, I pour'd forth tears in vain
To save your brother from the sacrifice;   164
But fierce Andronicus would not relent:
Therefore, away with her, and use her as you will:
The worse to her, the better lov'd of me.

    Lav. O Tamora! be call'd a gentle queen,   168
And with thine own hands kill me in this place;
For 'tis not life that I have begg'd so long;
Poor I was slain when Bassianus died.

    Tam. What begg'st thou, then? fond woman, let me
      go.   172

    Lav. 'Tis present death I beg; and one thing more
That womanhood denies my tongue to tell.
O keep me from their worse than killing lust,
And tumble me into some loathsome pit,   176
Where never man's eye may behold my body!
Do this, and be a charitable murderer.

    Tam. So should I rob my sweet sons of their fee:
No, let them satisfy their lust on thee.   180

    Dem. Away! for thou hast stay'd us here too long.

    Lav. No grace! no womanhood! Ah, beastly crea-
      ture,
The blot and enemy to our general name.
Confusion fall—   184

    Chi. Nay, then I'll stop your mouth. Bring thou
      her husband:
This is the hole where Aaron bid us hide him.

[*Demetrius throws the body of Bassianus into the pit;
     then exeunt Demetrius and Chiron, dragging off
     Lavinia.*]

172 fond: *foolish*   173 present: *instant*
183 blot . . . name: *a blot on, and enemy to, the good name of women
in general*

Tam. Farewell, my sons: see that you make her
    sure.
Ne'er let my heart know merry cheer indeed   188
Till all the Andronici be made away.
Now will I hence to seek my lovely Moor,
And let my spleenful sons this trull deflower.   *Exit.*

*Enter Aaron, with [Quintus and Martius,] two of
    Titus's Sons.*

Aar. Come on, my lords, the better foot before: 192
Straight will I bring you to the loathsome pit
Where I espied the panther fast asleep.
    Quin. My sight is very dull, whate'er it bodes.
    Mart. And mine, I promise you: were 't not for
        shame,   196
Well could I leave our sport to sleep awhile.

                        [*Falls into the pit.*]
    Quin. What! art thou fall'n? What subtle hole is
        this,
Whose mouth is cover'd with rude-growing briers,
Upon whose leaves are drops of new-shed blood   200
As fresh as morning's dew distill'd on flowers?
A very fatal place it seems to me.
Speak, brother, hast thou hurt thee with the fall?
    Mart. O brother! with the dismal'st object hurt   204
That ever eye with sight made heart lament.
    Aar. [*Aside.*] Now will I fetch the king to find them
        here,
That he thereby may give a likely guess
How these were they that made away his brother.   208
                        Exit Aaron.
    Mart. Why dost not comfort me, and help me out
From this unhallow'd and blood-stained hole?

191 spleenful: *hot, eager*   trull: *loose woman*

Quin. I am surprised with an uncouth fear;
A chilling sweat o'erruns my trembling joints: 212
My heart suspects more than mine eye can see.

Mart. To prove thou hast a true-divining heart,
Aaron and thou look down into this den,
And see a fearful sight of blood and death.   216

Quin. Aaron is gone; and my compassionate heart
Will not permit mine eyes once to behold
The thing whereat it trembles by surmise.
O tell me how it is! for ne'er till now   220
Was I a child, to fear I know not what.

Mart. Lord Bassianus lies embrewed here,
All on a heap, like to a slaughter'd lamb,
In this detested, dark, blood-drinking pit.   224

Quin. If it be dark, how dost thou know 'tis he?

Mart. Upon his bloody finger he doth wear
A precious ring, that lightens all the hole,
Which, like a taper in some monument,   228
Doth shine upon the dead man's earthy cheeks,
And shows the ragged entrails of the pit:
So pale did shine the moon on Pyramus
When he by night lay bath'd in maiden blood.   232
O brother! help me with thy fainting hand—
If fear hath made thee faint, as me it hath—
Out of this fell devouring receptacle,
As hateful as Cocytus' misty mouth.   236

Quin. Reach me thy hand, that I may help thee out;
Or, wanting strength to do thee so much good
I may be pluck'd into the swallowing womb
Of this deep pit, poor Bassianus' grave.   240
I have no strength to pluck thee to the brink.

211 uncouth: *strange, horrible*   222 embrewed: *soaked in blood*
223 on a heap: *in a heap*   227 A precious ring; *cf. n.*
231 Pyramus; *cf. n.*
236 Cocytus: *the river of lamentation in Hades*

Mart. Nor I no strength to climb without thy help.

Quin. Thy hand once more; I will not loose again,

Till thou art here aloft, or I below.   244

Thou canst not come to me: I come to thee.

> *Both fall in.*

Enter the Emperor, [with] Aaron the Moor.

Sat. Along with me: I'll see what hole is here,

And what he is that now is leap'd into it.

Say, who art thou that lately didst descend   248

Into this gaping hollow of the earth?

Mart. The unhappy son of old Andronicus;

Brought hither in a most unlucky hour,

To find thy brother Bassianus dead.   252

Sat. My brother dead! I know thou dost but jest:

He and his lady both are at the lodge,

Upon the north side of this pleasant chase;

'Tis not an hour since I left him there.   256

Mart. We know not where you left him all alive;

But, out alas! here have we found him dead.

*Enter Tamora [with Attendants], [Titus] Androni-
cus, and Lucius.*

Tam. Where is my lord, the king?

Sat. Here, Tamora; though griev'd with killing
grief.   260

Tam. Where is thy brother Bassianus?

Sat. Now to the bottom dost thou search my wound:

Poor Bassianus here lies murthered.

Tam. Then all too late I bring this fatal writ, 264

The complot of this timeless tragedy;

And wonder greatly that man's face can fold

243 loose: *loose my hold*   255 chase: *hunting-ground*
262 search: *probe*   265 complot: *plot*   timeless: *untimely*

In pleasing smiles such murderous tyranny.

*She giveth Saturnine a letter. Saturninus
reads the letter.*

Sat. 'And if we miss to meet him handsomely,   268
Sweet huntsman, Bassianus 'tis we mean,
Do thou so much as dig the grave for him:
Thou know'st our meaning.   Look for thy reward
Among the nettles at the elder-tree   272
Which overshades the mouth of that same pit
Where we decreed to bury Bassianus:
Do this, and purchase us thy lasting friends.'
O Tamora! was ever heard the like?   276
This is the pit, and this the elder-tree.
Look, sirs, if you can find the huntsman out
That should have murther'd Bassianus here.

Aar. My gracious lord, here is the bag of gold.   280

Sat. [*To Titus.*] Two of thy whelps, fell curs of
    bloody kind,
Have here bereft my brother of his life.
Sirs, drag them from the pit unto the prison:
There let them bide until we have devis'd   284
Some never-heard-of torturing pain for them.

Tam. What! are they in this pit?   O wondrous
    thing!
How easily murder is discovered!

Tit. High emperor, upon my feeble knee   288
I beg this boon with tears not lightly shed;
That this fell fault of my accursed sons,
Accursed, if the fault be prov'd in them,—

Sat. If it be prov'd! you see it is apparent.   292
Who found this letter?   Tamora, was it you?

Tam. Andronicus himself did take it up.

Tit. I did, my lord: yet let me be their bail;

274 decreed: *determined*

For, by my father's reverend tomb, I vow   296
They shall be ready at your highness' will
To answer their suspicion with their lives.

Sat. Thou shalt not bail them: see thou follow me.
Some bring the murther'd body, some the mur-
    therers: 300
Let them not speak a word; the guilt is plain;
For, by my soul, were there worse end than death,
That end upon them should be executed.

Tam. Andronicus, I will entreat the king: 304
Fear not thy sons, they shall do well enough.

Tit. Come, Lucius, come; stay not to talk with them.
                       Exeunt.

Scene Four

[*Another part of the Forest*]

*Enter the Empress's Sons, with Lavinia, her hands cut
off, and her tongue cut out, and ravished.*

Dem. So, now go tell, an if thy tongue can speak,
Who 'twas that cut thy tongue and ravish'd thee.

Chi. Write down thy mind, bewray thy meaning so;
An if thy stumps will let thee play the scribe.   4

Dem. See, how with signs and tokens she can
    scrowl.

Chi. Go home, call for sweet water, wash thy hands.

Dem. She hath no tongue to call, nor hands to wash;
And so let's leave her to her silent walks.   8

Chi. An 'twere my case, I should go hang myself.

Dem. If thou hadst hands to help thee knit the cord.
             Exeunt [*Demetrius and Chiron*].
                       Wind horns.

305 Fear not: *fear not for*   5 scrowl: *scrawl* (?); *cf. n.*
6 sweet: *perfumed*

Enter Marcus, from hunting, to Lavinia.

Mar. Who's this? my niece, that flies away so fast?
Cousin, a word; where is your husband?   12
If I do dream, would all my wealth would wake me!
If I do wake, some planet strike me down,
That I may slumber in eternal sleep!
Speak, gentle niece, what stern ungentle hands   16
Hath lopp'd and hew'd and made thy body bare
Of her two branches, those sweet ornaments,
Whose circling shadows kings have sought to sleep in,
And might not gain so great a happiness   20
As have thy love? Why dost not speak to me?
Alas! a crimson river of warm blood,
Like to a bubbling fountain stirr'd with wind,
Doth rise and fall between thy rosed lips,   24
Coming and going with thy honey breath.
But, sure, some Tereus hath deflower'd thee,
And, lest thou shouldst detect him, cut thy tongue.
Ah! now thou turn'st away thy face for shame;   28
And, notwithstanding all this loss of blood,
As from a conduit with three issuing spouts,
Yet do thy cheeks look red as Titan's face
Blushing to be encounter'd with a cloud.   32
Shall I speak for thee? shall I say 'tis so?
O that I knew thy heart! and knew the beast,
That I might rail at him to ease my mind.
Sorrow conceal'd, like to an oven stopp'd,   36
Doth burn the heart to cinders where it is.
Fair Philomela, she but lost her tongue,
And in a tedious sampler sew'd her mind:
But, lovely niece, that mean is cut from thee;   40

12 Cousin: *near relation, of either sex*   17 Hath: *have*
26 Tereus; *cf. n.*   31 Titan's: *the sun's*
34 thy heart: *what is in thy mind*   39 mind: *meaning; cf. n.*
40 mean: *means*

A craftier Tereus hast thou met withal,
And he hath cut those pretty fingers off,
That could have better sew'd than Philomel.
O! had the monster seen those lily hands   44
Tremble, like aspen-leaves, upon a lute,
And make the silken strings delight to kiss them,
He would not, then, have touch'd them for his life;
Or had he heard the heavenly harmony   48
Which that sweet tongue hath made,
He would have dropp'd his knife, and fell asleep,
As Cerberus at the Thracian poet's feet.
Come, let us go, and make thy father blind;   52
For such a sight will blind a father's eye:
One hour's storm will drown the fragrant meads;
What will whole months of tears thy father's eyes?
Do not draw back, for we will mourn with thee: 56
O could our mourning ease thy misery!   *Exeunt.*

ACT THIRD

Scene One

[Rome.   A Street]

*Enter the Judges and Senators [and Tribunes], with
    Titus's two Sons, bound, passing on the Stage to
    the place of execution; and Titus going before,
    pleading.*

Tit. Hear me, grave fathers! noble tribunes, stay!
For pity of mine age, whose youth was spent
In dangerous wars, whilst you securely slept;
For all my blood in Rome's great quarrel shed;   4
For all the frosty nights that I have watch'd;

51 Cerberus . . . feet; *cf. n.*

And for these bitter tears, which now you see
Filling the aged wrinkles in my cheeks:
Be pitiful to my condemned sons,   8
Whose souls are not corrupted as 'tis thought.
For two-and-twenty sons I never wept,
Because they died in honour's lofty bed.
For these, tribunes, in the dust I write   12

        Andronicus lieth down, and the Judges
                pass by him [and exeunt].

My heart's deep languor and my soul's sad tears.
Let my tears stanch the earth's dry appetite;
My sons' sweet blood will make it shame and blush.

        Exeunt [Senators, Tribunes, and the
           Others, with the Prisoners].

O earth! I will befriend thee more with rain,   16
That shall distil from these two ancient urns,
Than youthful April shall with all his showers:
In summer's drought I'll drop upon thee still;
In winter with warm tears I'll melt the snow,   20
And keep eternal spring-time on thy face,
So thou refuse to drink my dear sons' blood.

      Enter Lucius, with his weapon drawn.

O reverend tribunes! O gentle, aged men!
Unbind my sons, reverse the doom of death: 24
And let me say, that never wept before,
My tears are now prevailing orators.

  Luc. O noble father, you lament in vain:
The tribunes hear you not, no man is by;   28
And you recount your sorrows to a stone.

  Tit. Ah, Lucius, for thy brothers let me plead!
Grave tribunes, once more I entreat of you,—

10 two-and-twenty sons; *cf. n.*

Luc. My gracious lord, no tribune hears you
  speak.   32

Tit. Why, 'tis no matter, man: if they did hear,
They would not mark me, or if they did mark,
They would not pity me, yet plead I must,
And bootless, unto them.   36
Therefore I tell my sorrows to the stones,
Who, though they cannot answer my distress,
Yet in some sort they are better than the tribunes,
For that they will not intercept my tale.   40
When I do weep, they humbly at my feet
Receive my tears, and seem to weep with me;
And, were they but attired in grave weeds,
Rome could afford no tribune like to these.   44
A stone is as soft wax, tribunes more hard than stones;
A stone is silent, and offendeth not,
And tribunes with their tongues doom men to death.
                                            [*Rises.*]
But wherefore stand'st thou with thy weapon
  drawn?   48
Luc. To rescue my two brothers from their death;
For which attempt the judges have pronounc'd
My everlasting doom of banishment.

Tit. O happy man! they have befriended thee.   52
Why, foolish Lucius, dost thou not perceive
That Rome is but a wilderness of tigers?
Tigers must prey; and Rome affords no prey
But me and mine: how happy art thou then,   56
From these devourers to be banished!
But who comes with our brother Marcus here?

Enter Marcus and Lavinia.

Mar. Titus, prepare thy aged eyes to weep;

34-37 *Cf. n.*

Or, if not so, thy noble heart to break: 60
I bring consuming sorrow to thine age.

   Tit. Will it consume me? let me see it then.

   Mar. This was thy daughter.

   Tit. Why, Marcus, so she is.   64

   Luc. Ay me! this object kills me.

   Tit. Faint-hearted boy, arise, and look upon her.
Speak, Lavinia, what accursed hand
Hath made thee handless in thy father's sight?   68
What fool hath added water to the sea,
Or brought a faggot to bright-burning Troy?
My grief was at the height before thou cam'st;
And now, like Nilus, it disdaineth bounds.   72
Give me a sword, I'll chop off my hands too;
For they have fought for Rome, and all in vain;
And they have nurs'd this woe, in feeding life;
In bootless prayer have they been held up,   76
And they have serv'd me to effectless use:
Now all the service I require of them
Is that the one will help to cut the other.
'Tis well, Lavinia, that thou hast no hands,   80
For hands, to do Rome service, are but vain.

   Luc. Speak, gentle sister, who hath martyr'd thee?

   Mar. O! that delightful engine of her thoughts,
That blabb'd them with such pleasing eloquence,   84
Is torn from forth that pretty hollow cage,
Where, like a sweet melodious bird, it sung
Sweet varied notes, enchanting every ear.

   Luc. O! say thou for her, who hath done this
     deed?   88

   Mar. O! thus I found her straying in the park,
Seeking to hide herself, as doth the deer,

72 Nilus: *the river Nile*   77 effectless: *ineffectual*
83 engine: *instrument*

That hath receiv'd some unrecuring wound.

   Tit. It was my dear; and he that wounded her   92
Hath hurt me more than had he kill'd me dead:
For now I stand as one upon a rock
Environ'd with a wilderness of sea,
Who marks the waxing tide grow wave by wave,   96
Expecting ever when some envious surge
Will in his brinish bowels swallow him.
This way to death my wretched sons are gone;
Here stands my other son, a banish'd man,   100
And here my brother, weeping at my woes:
But that which gives my soul the greatest spurn,
Is dear Lavinia, dearer than my soul.
Had I but seen thy picture in this plight   104
It would have madded me: what shall I do
Now I behold thy lively body so?
Thou hast no hands to wipe away thy tears,
Nor tongue to tell me who hath martyr'd thee: 108
Thy husband he is dead, and for his death
Thy brothers are condemn'd, and dead by this.
Look, Marcus! ah! son Lucius, look on her:
When I did name her brothers, then fresh tears   112
Stood on her cheeks, as doth the honey-dew
Upon a gather'd lily almost wither'd.

   Mar. Perchance she weeps because they kill'd her
      husband;
Perchance because she knows them innocent.   116

   Tit. If they did kill thy husband, then be joyful,
Because the law hath ta'en revenge on them.
No, no, they would not do so foul a deed;
Witness the sorrow that their sister makes.   120
Gentle Lavinia, let me kiss thy lips;

91 unrecuring: *incurable*   97 envious: *malignant*
98 his: *its*   102 spurn: *pang*

Or make some sign how I may do thee ease.
Shall thy good uncle, and thy brother Lucius,
And thou, and I, sit round about some fountain,   124
Looking all downwards, to behold our cheeks
How they are stain'd, like meadows yet not dry,
With miry slime left on them by a flood?
And in the fountain shall we gaze so long   128
Till the fresh taste be taken from that clearness,
And made a brine-pit with our bitter tears?
Or shall we cut away our hands, like thine?
Or shall we bite our tongues, and in dumb shows   132
Pass the remainder of our hateful days?
What shall we do? let us, that have our tongues,
Plot some device of further misery,
To make us wonder'd at in time to come.   136

  Luc. Sweet father, cease your tears; for at your
   grief
See how my wretched sister sobs and weeps.
  Mar. Patience, dear niece. Good Titus, dry thine
   eyes.
  Tit. Ah, Marcus, Marcus, brother! well I wot   140
Thy napkin cannot drink a tear of mine,
For thou, poor man, hast drown'd it with thine own.
  Luc. Ah, my Lavinia, I will wipe thy cheeks.
  Tit. Mark, Marcus, mark! I understand her
   signs: 144
Had she a tongue to speak, now would she say
That to her brother which I said to thee:
His napkin, with his true tears all bewet,
Can do no service on her sorrowful cheeks.   148
O what a sympathy of woe is this!
As far from help as limbo is from bliss.

141 napkin: *handkerchief*   150 limbo: *i.e. hell; cf. n.*

Enter Aaron the Moor, alone.

Aar. Titus Andronicus, my lord the emperor
Sends thee this word: that, if thou love thy sons,   152
Let Marcus, Lucius, or thyself, old Titus,
Or any one of you, chop off your hand,
And send it to the king: he for the same
Will send thee hither both thy sons alive;   156
And that shall be the ransom for their fault.

Tit. O gracious emperor! O gentle Aaron!
Did ever raven sing so like a lark,
That gives sweet tidings of the sun's uprise?   160
With all my heart, I'll send the emperor my hand:
Good Aaron, wilt thou help to chop it off?

Luc. Stay, father! for that noble hand of thine,
That hath thrown down so many enemies,   164
Shall not be sent; my hand will serve the turn:
My youth can better spare my blood than you;
And therefore mine shall save my brothers' lives.

Mar. Which of your hands hath not defended
     Rome,   168
And rear'd aloft the bloody battle-axe,
Writing destruction on the enemy's castle?
O! none of both but are of high desert:
My hand hath been but idle; let it serve   172
To ransom my two nephews from their death;
Then have I kept it to a worthy end.

Aar. Nay, come, agree whose hand shall go along,
For fear they die before their pardon come.   176

Mar. My hand shall go.

Luc.   By heaven, it shall not go!

Tit. Sirs, strive no more: such wither'd herbs as
     these
Are meet for plucking up, and therefore mine.

170 the enemy's castle; *cf. n.*   171 both: *both of you*

Luc. Sweet father, if I shall be thought thy son, 180
Let me redeem my brothers both from death.

Mar. And for our father's sake, and mother's care,
Now let me show a brother's love to thee.

Tit. Agree between you; I will spare my hand.   184

Luc. Then I'll go fetch an axe.

Mar.   But I will use the axe.

      Exeunt [*Lucius and Marcus*].

Tit. Come hither, Aaron; I'll deceive them both:
Lend me thy hand, and I will give thee mine.

Aar. [*Aside.*] If that be call'd deceit, I will be
  honest,   188
And never, whilst I live, deceive men so:
But I'll deceive you in another sort,
And that you'll say, ere half an hour pass.

      He cuts off Titus's hand.

Enter Lucius and Marcus again.

Tit. Now stay your strife: what shall be is dis-
  patch'd.   192
Good Aaron, give his majesty my hand:
Tell him it was a hand that warded him
From thousand dangers; bid him bury it:
More hath it merited; that let it have.   196
As for my sons, say I account of them
As jewels purchas'd at an easy price;
And yet dear too, because I bought mine own.

Aar. I go, Andronicus; and for thy hand,   200
Look by and by to have thy sons with thee.
[*Aside.*] Their heads, I mean. O how this villainy
Doth fat me with the very thoughts of it!
Let fools do good, and fair men call for grace, 204
Aaron will have his soul black like his face.   *Exit.*

190 sort: *fashion*

Tit. O! here I lift this one hand up to heaven,
And bow this feeble ruin to the earth:
If any power pities wretched tears,   208
To that I call!—[*To Lavinia.*]—What! wilt thou
    kneel with me?
Do, then, dear heart; for heaven shall hear our
    prayers,
Or with our sighs we'll breathe the welkin dim,
And stain the sun with fog, as sometime clouds   212
When they do hug him in their melting bosoms.

Mar. O brother, speak with possibilities,
And do not break into these deep extremes.

Tit. Is not my sorrow deep, having no bottom?   216
Then be my passions bottomless with them.

Mar. But yet let reason govern thy lament.

Tit. If there were reason for these miseries,
Then into limits could I bind my woes.   220
When heaven doth weep, doth not the earth o'erflow?
If the winds rage, doth not the sea wax mad,
Threat'ning the welkin with his big-swoll'n face?
And wilt thou have a reason for this coil?   224
I am the sea; hark how her sighs do flow!
She is the weeping welkin, I the earth:
Then must my sea be moved with her sighs;
Then must my earth with her continual tears   228
Become a deluge, overflow'd and drown'd;
For why my bowels cannot hide her woes,
But like a drunkard must I vomit them.
Then give me leave, for losers will have leave   232
To ease their stomachs with their bitter tongues.

Enter a Messenger with two heads and a hand.

Mess. Worthy Andronicus, ill art thou repaid

211 welkin: *sky*   214 with: *within the range of*
224 coil: *confusion*   230 For why: *because*

For that good hand thou sent'st the emperor.
Here are the heads of thy two noble sons,   236
And here's thy hand, in scorn to thee sent back:
Thy griefs their sports, thy resolution mock'd;
That woe is me to think upon thy woes,
More than remembrance of my father's death.   240
                                                    Exit.

   Mar. Now let hot Ætna cool in Sicily,
And be my heart an ever-burning hell!
These miseries are more than may be borne.
To weep with them that weep doth ease some deal, 244
But sorrow flouted at is double death.

   Luc. Ah! that this sight should make so deep a
         wound,
And yet detested life not shrink thereat!
That ever death should let life bear his name,   248
Where life hath no more interest but to breathe!
                        [*Lavinia kisses Titus.*]

   Mar. Alas! poor heart; that kiss is comfortless
As frozen water to a starved snake.

   Tit. When will this fearful slumber have an end? 252

   Mar. Now, farewell, flattery: die, Andronicus;
Thou dost not slumber: see, thy two sons' heads,
Thy warlike hand, thy mangled daughter here;
Thy other banish'd son, with this dear sight   256
Struck pale and bloodless; and thy brother, I,
Even like a stony image, cold and numb.
Ah! now no more will I control my griefs.
Rent off thy silver hair, thy other hand   260
Gnawing with thy teeth; and be this dismal sight
The closing up of our most wretched eyes!

239 That: *so that*   244 some deal: *somewhat; cf. n.*
251 starved: *benumbed with cold*
256 dear sight: *a sight that touches him very closely*
260 Rent: *rend*

Now is a time to storm; why art thou still?
  Tit. Ha, ha, ha! 264
  Mar. Why dost thou laugh? it fits not with this hour.
  Tit. Why, I have not another tear to shed:
Besides, this sorrow is an enemy,
And would usurp upon my watery eyes, 268
And make them blind with tributary tears:
Then which way shall I find Revenge's cave?
For these two heads do seem to speak to me,
And threat me I shall never come to bliss 272
Till all these mischiefs be return'd again
Even in their throats that have committed them.
Come, let me see what task I have to do.
You heavy people, circle me about, 276
That I may turn me to each one of you,
And swear unto my soul to right your wrongs.
The vow is made. Come, brother, take a head;
And in this hand the other will I bear. 280
Lavinia, thou shalt be employ'd in these things:
Bear thou my hand, sweet wench, between thy teeth.
As for thee, boy, go get thee from my sight;
Thou art an exile, and thou must not stay: 284
Hie to the Goths, and raise an army there:
And if you love me, as I think you do,
Let's kiss and part, for we have much to do.
                         Exeunt. Manet Lucius.
  Luc. Farewell, Andronicus, my noble father; 288
The woefull'st man that ever liv'd in Rome:
Farewell, proud Rome; till Lucius come again,
He leaves his pledges dearer than his life.
Farewell, Lavinia, my noble sister; 292
O would thou wert as thou tofore hast been!
But now nor Lucius nor Lavinia lives

276 heavy: *sorrowful*   293 tofore: *heretofore*

But in oblivion and hateful griefs.
If Lucius live, he will requite your wrongs,   296
And make proud Saturnine and his empress
Beg at the gates like Tarquin and his queen.
Now will I to the Goths, and raise a power,
To be reveng'd on Rome and Saturnine.   300

Exit Lucius.

Scene Two

[*The Same.   A Room in Titus's House*]   *A Banquet*
[*set out*]

Enter Andronicus, Marcus, Lavinia, and the Boy
[*young Lucius*].

Tit. So, so; now sit; and look you eat no more
Than will preserve just so much strength in us
As will revenge these bitter woes of ours.
Marcus, unknit that sorrow-wreathen knot: 4
Thy niece and I, poor creatures, want our hands,
And cannot passionate our ten-fold grief
With folded arms.   This poor right hand of mine
Is left to tyrannize upon my breast;   8
Who, when my heart, all mad with misery,
Beats in this hollow prison of my flesh,
Then thus I thump it down.
[*To Lavinia.*] Thou map of woe, that thus dost talk
    in signs!   12
When thy poor heart beats with outrageous beating
Thou canst not strike it thus to make it still.
Wound it with sighing, girl, kill it with groans;
Or get some little knife between thy teeth,   16

299 power: *army*   Scene Two; *cf. n.*
4 sorrow-wreathen knot; *cf. n.*   12 map: *picture*
15 Wound it with sighing; *cf. n.*

And just against thy heart make thou a hole;
That all the tears that thy poor eyes let fall
May run into that sink, and, soaking in,
Drown the lamenting fool in sea-salt tears.   20

Mar. Fie, brother, fie! teach her not thus to lay
Such violent hands upon her tender life.

Tit. How now! has sorrow made thee dote already?
Why, Marcus, no man should be mad but I.   24
What violent hands can she lay on her life?
Ah! wherefore dost thou urge the name of hands?
To bid Æneas tell the tale twice o'er,
How Troy was burnt and he made miserable?   28
O handle not the theme, to talk of hands,
Lest we remember still that we have none!
Fie, fie! how franticly I square my talk,
As if we should forget we had no hands,   32
If Marcus did not name the word of hands.
Come, let's fall to; and, gentle girl, eat this:
Here is no drink.   Hark, Marcus, what she says;
I can interpret all her martyr'd signs: 36
She says she drinks no other drink but tears,
Brew'd with her sorrow, mash'd upon her cheeks.
Speechless complainer, I will learn thy thought;
In thy dumb action will I be as perfect   40
As begging hermits in their holy prayers:
Thou shalt not sigh, nor hold thy stumps to heaven,
Nor wink, nor nod, nor kneel, nor make a sign,
But I of these will wrest an alphabet,   44
And by still practice learn to know thy meaning.

Boy. Good grandsire, leave these bitter deep laments:

31 square: *shape, fashion*
36 martyr'd signs: *signs of her martyrdom*
38 Brew'd . . . mash'd; *cf. n.*
40 be as perfect: *show as perfect an understanding*
44 of these: *from these*   45 still: *constant*

Make my aunt merry with some pleasing tale.

    Mar. Alas! the tender boy, in passion mov'd,   48
Doth weep to see his grandsire's heaviness.

    Tit. Peace, tender sapling; thou art made of tears,
And tears will quickly melt thy life away.

                  Marcus strikes the dish with a knife.
What dost thou strike at, Marcus, with thy knife? 52

    Mar. At that that I have kill'd, my lord,—a fly.

    Tit. Out on thee, murderer! thou kill'st my heart;
Mine eyes are cloy'd with view of tyranny:
A deed of death, done on the innocent,   56
Becomes not Titus' brother. Get thee gone;
I see thou art not for my company.

    Mar. Alas! my lord, I have but kill'd a fly.

    Tit. 'But!'   How, if that fly had a father and
        mother?   60
How would he hang his slender gilded wings
And buzz lamenting doings in the air!
Poor harmless fly,
That, with his pretty buzzing melody,   64
Came here to make us merry! and thou hast kill'd him.

    Mar. Pardon me, sir; it was a black ill-favour'd fly,
Like to the empress' Moor; therefore I kill'd him.

    Tit. O, O, O!   68
Then pardon me for reprehending thee,
For thou hast done a charitable deed.
Give me thy knife, I will insult on him;
Flattering myself, as if it were the Moor   72
Come hither purposely to poison me.
There's for thyself, and that's for Tamora.
Ah, sirrah!
Yet I think we are not brought so low,   76

62 lamenting doings: *stories of lamentable deeds*
71 insult on: *exult over*
76 Yet . . . low: *we are not yet brought so low*

But that between us we can kill a fly
That comes in likeness of a coal-black Moor.

   Mar. Alas, poor man! grief has so wrought on him,
He takes false shadows for true substances.   80

   Tit. Come, take away. Lavinia, go with me:
I'll to thy closet; and go read with thee
Sad stories chanced in the times of old.
Come, boy, and go with me: thy sight is young,   84
And thou shalt read when mine begin to dazzle.

                         Exeunt.

ACT FOURTH

Scene One

[*Rome. Titus's Garden*]

*Enter young Lucius, and Lavinia running after him,
and the Boy flies from her, with his books under
his arm. [Then] enter Titus and Marcus.*

   Boy. Help, grandsire, help! my aunt Lavinia
Follows me everywhere, I know not why.
Good uncle Marcus, see how swift she comes:
Alas, sweet aunt! I know not what you mean.   4

   Mar. Stand by me, Lucius; do not fear thine aunt.

   Tit. She loves thee, boy, too well to do thee harm.

   Boy. Ay, when my father was in Rome, she did.

   Mar. What means my niece Lavinia by these
signs?   8

   Tit. Fear her not, Lucius: somewhat doth she mean.
See, Lucius, see how much she makes of thee;
Somewhither would she have thee   with her.
Ah, boy! Cornelia never with more care   12

81 take away: *clear the table*   85 mine: *mine eyes*
12 Cornelia: *the mother of the Gracchi*

Read to her sons, than she hath read to thee
Sweet poetry and Tully's Orator.

   [*Mar.*] Canst thou not guess wherefore she plies
thee thus?

   Boy. My lord, I know not, I, nor can I guess,   16
Unless some fit or frenzy do possess her;
For I have heard my grandsire say full oft,
Extremity of griefs would make men mad;
And I have read that Hecuba of Troy   20
Ran mad through sorrow; that made me to fear,
Although, my lord, I know my noble aunt
Loves me as dear as e'er my mother did,
And would not, but in fury, fright my youth;   24
Which made me down to throw my books and fly,
Causeless, perhaps. But pardon me, sweet aunt;
And, madam, if my uncle Marcus go,
I will most willingly attend your ladyship.   28

   Mar. Lucius, I will.

               [*Lavinia turns over with her stumps the
                books which Lucius has let fall.*]

   Tit. How now, Lavinia! Marcus, what means this?
Some book there is that she desires to see.
Which is it, girl, of these? Open them, boy.   32
But thou art deeper read, and better skill'd;
Come, and take choice of all my library,
And so beguile thy sorrow, till the heavens
Reveal the damn'd contriver of this deed.   36
Why lifts she up her arms in sequence thus?

   Mar. I think she means that there was more than
    one
Confederate in the fact: ay, more there was;
Or else to heaven she heaves them for revenge.   40

14 Tully's Orator: *Cicero's De Oratore*   15 plies: *importunes*
20, 21 Hecuba . . . sorrow; *cf. n.*   24 fury: *madness*
37 in sequence: *one after the other; cf. n.*   39 fact: *deed*

Tit. Lucius, what book is that she tosseth so?

Boy. Grandsire, 'tis Ovid's Metamorphoses;
My mother gave it me.

Mar.   For love of her that's gone,
Perhaps, she cull'd it from among the rest.   44

Tit. Soft! so busily she turns the leaves! Help her.
What would she find? Lavinia, shall I read?
This is the tragic tale of Philomel,
And treats of Tereus' treason and his rape;   48
And rape, I fear, was root of thine annoy.

Mar. See, brother, see! note how she quotes the
     leaves.

Tit. Lavinia, wert thou thus surpris'd, sweet girl,
Ravish'd and wrong'd, as Philomela was,   52
Forc'd in the ruthless, vast, and gloomy woods?
See, see!
Ay, such a place there is, where we did hunt,—
O had we never, never hunted there!—   56
Pattern'd by that the poet here describes,
By nature made for murthers and for rapes.

Mar. O! why should nature build so foul a den,
Unless the gods delight in tragedies?   60

Tit. Give signs, sweet girl, for here are none but
     friends,
What Roman lord it was durst do the deed:
Or slunk not Saturnine, as Tarquin erst,
That left the camp to sin in Lucrece' bed?   64

Mar. Sit down, sweet niece: brother, sit down by
     me.
Apollo, Pallas, Jove, or Mercury,
Inspire me, that I may this treason find!
My lord, look here; look here, Lavinia: 68

47 Philomel; *cf. n. on* II. iii. 43   49 annoy: *suffering*
50 quotes: *examines*   57 Pattern'd by: *fashioned after*
63 erst: *formerly*

This sandy plot is plain; guide, if thou canst,
This after me.

> *He writes his name with his staff, and*
> *guides it with feet and mouth.*

I have writ my name
Without the help of any hand at all.
Curs'd be that heart that forc'd us to this shift!   72
Write thou, good niece, and here display at last
What God will have discover'd for revenge.
Heaven guide thy pen to print thy sorrows plain,
That we may know the traitors and the truth!   76

> *She takes the staff in her mouth, and*
> *guides it with her stumps, and writes.*

Tit. O! do ye read, my lord, what she hath writ?
'Stuprum, Chiron, Demetrius.'

Mar. What, what! the lustful sons of Tamora
Performers of this heinous, bloody deed?   80

Tit. Magni dominator poli,
Tam lentus audis scelera? tam lentus vides?

Mar. O calm thee, gentle lord! although I know
There is enough written upon this earth   84
To stir a mutiny in the mildest thoughts
And arm the minds of infants to exclaims.
My lord, kneel down with me; Lavinia, kneel;
And kneel, sweet boy, the Roman Hector's hope;   88
And swear with me, as, with the woeful fere
And father of that chaste dishonour'd dame,
Lord Junius Brutus sware for Lucrece' rape,
That we will prosecute by good advice   92
Mortal revenge upon these traitorous Goths,
And see their blood, or die with this reproach.

78 Stuprum: *rape*
81 Magni dominator, etc.: *Ruler of the great heaven, dost thou so*
   calmly hear crimes, so calmly look upon them? Cf. n.
86 exclaims: *exclamations*
87-91 My lord, kneel down, etc.; *cf. n.*   89 fere: *mate*

Tit. 'Tis sure enough, an you knew how;
But if you hunt these bear-whelps, then beware: 96
The dam will wake, an if she wind you once:
She's with the lion deeply still in league,
And lulls him whilst she playeth on her back,
And when he sleeps will she do what she list.   100
You're a young huntsman, Marcus; let it alone;
And, come, I will go get a leaf of brass,
And with a gad of steel will write these words,
And lay it by: the angry northern wind   104
Will blow these sands like Sibyl's leaves abroad,
And where's your lesson then?   Boy, what say you?

Boy. I say, my lord, that if I were a man,
Their mother's bed-chamber should not be safe   108
For these bad bondmen to the yoke of Rome.

Mar. Ay, that's my boy! thy father hath full oft
For his ungrateful country done the like.

Boy. And, uncle, so will I, an if I live.   112

Tit. Come, go with me into mine armoury:
Lucius, I'll fit thee; and withal my boy
Shall carry from me to the empress' sons
Presents that I intend to send them both: 116
Come, come! thou'lt do thy message, wilt thou not?

Boy. Ay, with my dagger in their bosoms, grand-
    sire.

Tit. No, boy, not so; I'll teach thee another course.
Lavinia, come.   Marcus, look to my house;   120
Lucius and I'll go brave it at the court:
Ay, marry, will we, sir; and we'll be waited on.
                Exeunt [*Titus, Lavinia, and young Lucius*].

Mar. O heavens! can you hear a good man groan,
And not relent or not compassion him?   124

97 wind: *scent*   103 gad: *point*
105 Sibyl's leaves; *cf. n.*   124 compassion: *have compassion on*

Marcus, attend him in his ecstasy,
That hath more scars of sorrow in his heart
Than foemen's marks upon his batter'd shield;
But yet so just that he will not revenge.　128
Revenge the heavens for old Andronicus!　*Exit.*

Scene Two

[The same.　A Room in the Palace]

*Enter Aaron, Chiron, and Demetrius at one door; and
　at another door young Lucius and another, with
　a bundle of weapons, and verses writ upon them.*

Chi. Demetrius, here's the son of Lucius;
He hath some message to deliver us.

Aar. Ay, some mad message from his mad grand-
　father.

Boy. My lords, with all the humbleness I may,　4
I greet your honours from Andronicus;

[Aside.] And pray the Roman gods, confound you
　both!

Dem. Gramercy, lovely Lucius: what's the news?

Boy. [Aside.] That you are both decipher'd, that's
　the news,　8
For villains mark'd with rape. *[Aloud.]* May it please
　you,
My grandsire, well advis'd, hath sent by me
The goodliest weapons of his armoury,
To gratify your honourable youth,　12
The hope of Rome, for so he bade me say;
And so I do, and with his gifts present
Your lordships, that whenever you have need,

125 ecstasy: *frenzy*　　　10 well-advis'd: *in his right mind*

You may be armed and appointed well. 16
And so I leave you both: [*Aside.*] like bloody villains.
                        Exit [*with Attendant*].

   Dem. What's here?   A scroll, and written round
     about?
Let's see:——
[*Reads.*] '*Integer vitæ, scelerisque purus,* 20
         Non eget Mauri jaculis, nec arcu.'
   Chi. O! 'tis a verse in Horace; I know it well:
I read it in the grammar long ago.
   Aar. Ay, just, a verse in Horace; right, you have
     it. 24
[*Aside.*] Now, what a thing it is to be an ass!
Here's no sound jest! the old man hath found their
     guilt
And sends them weapons wrapp'd about with lines,
That wound, beyond their feeling, to the quick; 28
But were our witty empress well afoot,
She would applaud Andronicus' conceit:
But let her rest in her unrest awhile.
[*To them.*] And now, young lords, was 't not a happy
     star 32
Led us to Rome, strangers and more than so,
Captives, to be advanced to this height?
It did me good before the palace gate
To brave the tribune in his brother's hearing. 36
   Dem. But me more good, to see so great a lord
Basely insinuate and send us gifts.
   Aar. Had he not reason, Lord Demetrius?
Did you not use his daughter very friendly? 40
   Dem. I would we had a thousand Roman dames
At such a bay, by turn to serve our lust.

16 appointed: *equipped*   20 Integer vitæ, etc.; *cf. n.*
24 just: *just so*   26 sound jest; *cf. n.*
42 At such a bay: *under such circumstances*

Chi. A charitable wish and full of love.

Aar. Here lacks but your mother for to say amen. 44

Chi. And that would she for twenty thousand more.

Dem. Come, let us go and pray to all the gods
For our beloved mother in her pains.

Aar. [*Aside.*] Pray to the devils; the gods have
    given us over.   *Flourish* [*within*]. 48

Dem. Why do the emperor's trumpets flourish thus?

Chi. Belike, for joy the emperor hath a son.

Dem. Soft! who comes here?

     Enter Nurse with a blackamoor Child.

Nur. Good morrow, lords. O! tell me, did you
    see   52
Aaron the Moor?

Aar. Well, more or less, or ne'er a whit at all,
Here Aaron is; and what with Aaron now?

Nur. O gentle Aaron! we are all undone.   56
Now help, or woe betide thee evermore!

Aar. Why, what a caterwauling dost thou keep!
What dost thou wrap and fumble in thine arms?

Nur. O! that which I would hide from heaven's
    eye,   60
Our empress' shame, and stately Rome's disgrace!
She is deliver'd, lords, she is deliver'd.

Aar. To whom?

Nur.   I mean, she is brought a-bed.

Aar. Well, God give her good rest! What hath he
    sent her?   64

Nur. A devil.

Aar. Why, then she's the devil's dam: a joyful issue.

Nur. A joyless, dismal, black, and sorrowful issue.
Here is the babe, as loathsome as a toad   68

50 Belike: *probably*

Amongst the fairest breeders of our clime.
The empress sends it thee, thy stamp, thy seal,
And bids thee christen it with thy dagger's point.

Aar. 'Zounds, ye whore! is black so base a hue?　72
Sweet blowse, you are a beauteous blossom, sure.

Dem. Villain, what hast thou done?

Aar. That which thou canst not undo.

Chi. Thou hast undone our mother.　76

[*Aar.* Villain, I have done thy mother.]

Dem. And therein, hellish dog, thou hast undone.
Woe to her chance, and damn'd her loathed choice!
Accurs'd the offspring of so foul a fiend!　80

Chi. It shall not live.

Aar. It shall not die.

Nur. Aaron, it must; the mother wills it so.

Aar. What! must it, nurse? then let no man but
I　84
Do execution on my flesh and blood.

Dem. I'll broach the tadpole on my rapier's point:
Nurse, give it me; my sword shall soon dispatch it.

Aar. Sooner this sword shall plough thy bowels
up.　88
[*Takes the Child from the Nurse, and draws.*]
Stay, murtherous villains! will you kill your brother?
Now, by the burning tapers of the sky,
That shone so brightly when this boy was got,
He dies upon my scimitar's sharp point　92
That touches this my first-born son and heir.
I tell you, younglings, not Enceladus,
With all his threat'ning band of Typhon's brood,
Nor great Alcides, nor the god of war,　96
Shall seize this prey out of his father's hands.

72 'Zounds; *cf. n.*　　　73 blowse; *cf. n.*　　　86 broach: *spit*
94 Enceladus: *one of the Titans confined under Mt. Ætna*
95 Typhon's brood; *cf. n.*　　　96 Alcides: *Hercules*

What, what, ye sanguine, shallow-hearted boys!
Ye white-lim'd walls! ye alehouse painted signs!
Coal-black is better than another hue,   100
In that it scorns to bear another hue;
For all the water in the ocean
Can never turn the swan's black legs to white,
Although she lave them hourly in the flood.   104
Tell the empress from me, I am of age
To keep mine own, excuse it how she can.

 Dem. Wilt thou betray thy noble mistress thus?

 Aar. My mistress is my mistress; this myself;   108
The vigour, and the picture of my youth:
This before all the world do I prefer;
This maugre all the world will I keep safe,
Or some of you shall smoke for it in Rome.   112

 Dem. By this our mother is for ever sham'd.

 Chi. Rome will despise her for this foul escape.

 Nur. The emperor in his rage will doom her death.

 Chi. I blush to think upon this ignomy.   116

 Aar. Why, there's the privilege your beauty bears.
Fie, treacherous hue! that will betray with blushing
The close enacts and counsels of the heart.
Here's a young lad fram'd of another leer: 120
Look how the black slave smiles upon the father,
As who should say, 'Old lad, I am thine own.'
He is your brother, lords, sensibly fed
Of that self blood that first gave life to you;   124
And from that womb where you imprison'd were
He is enfranchised and come to light:
Nay, he is your brother by the surer side,
Although my seal be stamped in his face.   128

---

98 sanguine: *blood-colored*   99 white-lim'd: *whitewashed*
104 lave: *wash*   111 maugre: *in spite of*
114 escape: *escapade*   116 ignomy: *ignominy*
119 enacts: *workings*   120 leer: *complexion*
123 sensibly: *manifestly*   124 self: *selfsame*

Nur. Aaron, what shall I say unto the empress?

Dem. Advise thee, Aaron, what is to be done,
And we will all subscribe to thy advice:
Save thou the child, so we may all be safe.   132

Aar. Then sit we down, and let us all consult.
My son and I will have the wind of you:
Keep there; now talk at pleasure of your safety.

[*They sit.*]

Dem. How many women saw this child of his?   136

Aar. Why, so, brave lords! when we join in league,
I am a lamb; but if you brave the Moor,
The chafed boar, the mountain lioness,
The ocean swells not so as Aaron storms.   140
But say, again, how many saw the child?

Nur. Cornelia the midwife, and myself,
And no one else but the deliver'd empress.

Aar. The empress, the midwife, and yourself: 144
Two may keep counsel when the third's away:
Go to the empress; tell her this I said:

He kills her.

'Weke, weke!'
So cries a pig prepared to the spit.   148

Dem. What mean'st thou, Aaron? Wherefore didst
thou this?

Aar. O Lord, sir, 'tis a deed of policy:
Shall she live to betray this guilt of ours,
A long-tongu'd babbling gossip? no, lords, no.   152
And now be it known to you my full intent.
Not far, one Muli lives, my countryman;
His wife but yesternight was brought to bed.
His child is like to her, fair as you are: 156
Go pack with him, and give the mother gold,

---

130 Advise thee: *consider*
134 have the wind of you: *keep an eye upon you*
154 one Muli lives; *cf. n.*   157 pack: *plot*

And tell them both the circumstance of all,
And how by this their child shall be advanc'd,
And be received for the emperor's heir,   160
And substituted in the place of mine,
To calm this tempest whirling in the court;
And let the emperor dandle him for his own.
Hark ye, lords; ye see, I have given her physic,   164
                        [*Pointing to the Nurse.*]
And you must needs bestow her funeral;
The fields are near, and you are gallant grooms.
This done, see that you take no longer days,
But send the midwife presently to me.   168
The midwife and the nurse well made away,
Then let the ladies tattle what they please.
    Chi. Aaron, I see thou wilt not trust the air
With secrets.
    Dem.   For this care of Tamora,   172
Herself and hers are highly bound to thee.
                Exeunt [*Demetrius and Chiron, bearing
                       off the Nurse's body*].
    Aar. Now to the Goths, as swift as swallow flies:
There to dispose this treasure in mine arms,
And secretly to greet the empress' friends.   176
Come on, you thick-lipp'd slave, I'll bear you hence;
For it is you that puts us to our shifts:
I'll make you feed on berries and on roots,
And feed on curds and whey, and suck the goat,   180
And cabin in a cave, and bring you up
To be a warrior, and command a camp.   *Exit.*

158 circumstance of all: *all the details*
165 bestow her funeral: *give her burial*
167 no longer days: *no more time*
168 presently: *instantly*   175 dispose: *dispose of*

Scene Three

[The same.   A Public Place]

*Enter Titus, old Marcus, young Lucius, and other
    gentlemen, [Publius, Sempronius, and Caius]
    with bows; and Titus bears the arrows, with
    letters on the ends of them.*

Tit. Come, Marcus, come; kinsmen, this is the way.
Sir boy, let me see your archery:
Look ye draw home enough, and 'tis there straight.
Terras Astræa reliquit: 4
Be you remember'd, Marcus, she's gone, she's fled.
Sirs, take you to your tools.   You, cousins, shall
Go sound the ocean, and cast your nets;
Haply you may find her in the sea;   8
Yet there's as little justice as at land.
No; Publius and Sempronius, you must do it;
'Tis you must dig with mattock and with spade,
And pierce the inmost centre of the earth: 12
Then, when you come to Pluto's region,
I pray you, deliver him this petition;
Tell him, it is for justice and for aid,
And that it comes from old Andronicus,   16
Shaken with sorrows in ungrateful Rome.
Ah, Rome!   Well, well; I made thee miserable
What time I threw the people's suffrages
On him that thus doth tyrannize o'er me.   20
Go, get you gone; and pray be careful all,
And leave you not a man-of-war unsearch'd:
This wicked emperor may have shipp'd her hence;
And, kinsmen, then we may go pipe for justice.   24

4 Terras Astræa reliquit: *Astræa has left the earth; cf. n.*
5 Be you remember'd: *be mindful*
13 Pluto's region: *the infernal regions*   24 pipe: *whistle*

Mar. O Publius! is not this a heavy case,
To see thy noble uncle thus distract?

Pub. Therefore, my lord, it highly us concerns
By day and night to attend him carefully,   28
And feed his humour kindly as we may,
Till time beget some careful remedy.

Mar. Kinsmen, his sorrows are past remedy.
Join with the Goths, and with revengeful war   32
Take wreak on Rome for this ingratitude,
And vengeance on the traitor Saturnine.

Tit. Publius, how now! how now, my masters!
What! have you met with her?   36

Pub. No, my good lord; but Pluto sends you word,
If you will have Revenge from hell, you shall:
Marry, for Justice, she is so employ'd,
He thinks, with Jove in heaven, or somewhere else, 40
So that perforce you must needs stay a time.

Tit. He doth me wrong to feed me with delays.
I'll dive into the burning lake below,
And pull her out of Acheron by the heels.   44
Marcus, we are but shrubs, no cedars we;
No big-bon'd men fram'd of the Cyclops' size;
But metal, Marcus, steel to the very back,
Yet wrung with wrongs more than our backs can
　　　　bear: 48
And sith there's no justice in earth nor hell,
We will solicit heaven and move the gods
To send down Justice for to wreak our wrongs.
Come, to this gear.　You are a good archer, Marcus. 52
　　　　　　　　　　　He gives them the arrows.

30 careful remedy: *remedy obtained through the exercise of care* (?)
33 wreak: *revenge*   39 for: *as for*
43, 44 burning lake . . . Acheron; *cf. n.*
46 Cyclops: *giants, servants of Vulcan*
51 wreak: *revenge*   52 gear: *business*

Ad Jovem, that's for you: here, *ad Apollinem:*
Ad Martem, that's for myself:
Here, boy, to Pallas: here, to Mercury:
To Saturn, Caius, not to Saturnine;　　　　　56
You were as good to shoot against the wind.
To it, boy!　Marcus, loose when I bid.
Of my word, I have written to effect;
There's not a god left unsolicited.　　　　　60

　　Mar. Kinsmen, shoot all your shafts into the court:
We will afflict the emperor in his pride.

　　Tit. Now, masters, draw. [*They shoot.*] O! well
　　　　said, Lucius!
Good boy, in Virgo's lap: give it Pallas.　　　64

　　Mar. My lord, I aim a mile beyond the moon;
Your letter is with Jupiter by this.

　　Tit. Ha, ha! Publius, Publius, what hast thou done?
See, see! thou hast shot off one of Taurus' horns.　68

　　Mar. This was the sport, my lord: when Publius
　　　　shot,
The Bull, being gall'd, gave Aries such a knock
That down fell both the Ram's horns in the court;
And who should find them but the empress' villain?　72
She laugh'd, and told the Moor, he should not choose
But give them to his master for a present.

　　Tit. Why, there it goes: God give his lordship joy!

Enter the Clown, with a basket, and two pigeons in it.

News! news from heaven!　Marcus, the post is
　　come.　　　　　　　　　　　　　　　76
Sirrah, what tidings? have you any letters?
Shall I have justice? what says Jupiter?

53, 54 Ad Jovem, etc.: *to Jupiter, to Apollo, to Mars*
58 loose: *shoot*
59 Of my word: *upon my word*　　　　to effect: *to the purpose*
63 well said: *well done*
64-70 Virgo . . . Taurus . . . Aries: *constellations; cf. n.*

Clo. O! the gibbet-maker? He says that he
hath taken them down again, for the man must 80
not be hanged till the next week.

Tit. But what says Jupiter, I ask thee?

Clo. Alas! sir, I know not Jupiter; I never
drank with him in all my life. 84

Tit. Why, villain, art not thou the carrier?

Clo. Ay, of my pigeons, sir; nothing else.

Tit. Why, didst thou not come from heaven?

Clo. From heaven! alas! sir, I never came 88
there. God forbid I should be so bold to press
to heaven in my young days. Why, I am going
with my pigeons to the tribunal plebs, to take
up a matter of brawl betwixt my uncle and one 92
of the emperial's men.

Mar. Why, sir, that is as fit as can be to
serve for your oration; and let him deliver the
pigeons to the emperor from you. 96

Tit. Tell me, can you deliver an oration to
the emperor with a grace?

Clo. Nay, truly, sir, I could never say grace
in all my life. 100

Tit. Sirrah, come hither: make no more ado,
But give your pigeons to the emperor:
By me thou shalt have justice at his hands.
Hold, hold; meanwhile, here's money for thy
    charges. 104
Give me pen and ink.
Sirrah, can you with a grace deliver a supplication?

Clo. Ay, sir.

Tit. Then here is a supplication for you. 108
And when you come to him, at the first ap-

---

91 tribunal plebs: *tribune of the people* (*properly, tribunus plebis*)
91, 92 take up: *make up*   93 emperial's: *emperor's*

proach you must kneel; then kiss his foot; then
deliver up your pigeons; and then look for your
reward. I'll be at hand, sir; see you do it bravely. 112

    Clo. I warrant you, sir; let me alone.

    Tit. Sirrah, hast thou a knife? Come, let me see
    it.

Here, Marcus, fold it in the oration;
For thou hast made it like an humble suppliant: 116
And when thou hast given it the emperor,
Knock at my door, and tell me what he says.

    Clo. God be with you, sir; I will.   *Exit.*

    Tit. Come, Marcus, let us go. Publius, follow me. 120
                                Exeunt.

Scene Four

[*The Same. Before the Palace*]

*Enter the Emperor and Empress, and her two Sons
    [Lords and Others]. The Emperor brings the
    arrows in his hand that Titus shot at him.*

    Sat. Why, lords, what wrongs are these! Was ever
    seen

An emperor in Rome thus overborne,
Troubled, confronted thus; and, for the extent
Of egal justice, us'd in such contempt?   4
My lords, you know, [as do] the mightful gods,—
However these disturbers of our peace
Buzz in the people's ears,—there nought hath pass'd,
But even with law, against the wilful sons   8
Of old Andronicus. And what an if
His sorrows have so overwhelm'd his wits,

112 bravely: *in good style*
3, 4 extent Of egal justice: *maintenance of equal justice*
7 Buzz: *whisper*   8 even with: *in accord with*

Shall we be thus afflicted in his wreaks,

His fits, his frenzy, and his bitterness?   12

And now he writes to heaven for his redress:

See, here's to Jove, and this to Mercury;

This to Apollo; this to the god of war;

Sweet scrolls to fly about the streets of Rome!   16

What's this but libelling against the senate,

And blazoning our injustice everywhere?

A goodly humour, is it not, my lords?

As who would say, in Rome no justice were.   20

But if I live, his feigned ecstasies

Shall be no shelter to these outrages;

But he and his shall know that justice lives

In Saturninus' health; whom, if she sleep,   24

He'll so awake, as she in fury shall

Cut off the proud'st conspirator that lives.

   Tam. My gracious lord, my lovely Saturnine,

Lord of my life, commander of my thoughts,   28

Calm thee, and bear the faults of Titus' age,

Th' effects of sorrow for his valiant sons,

Whose loss hath pierc'd him deep and scarr'd his
    heart;

And rather comfort his distressed plight   32

Than prosecute the meanest or the best

For these contempts.—[*Aside.*] Why, thus it shall be-
    come

High-witted Tamora to gloze with all:

But, Titus, I have touch'd thee to the quick,   36

Thy life-blood out: if Aaron now be wise,

Then is all safe, the anchor's in the port.

Enter Clown.

How now, good fellow! wouldst thou speak with us?

11 wreaks: *revenges*   21 ecstasies: *insanity*
25 as: *that*   35 High-witted: *cunning*   gloze: *beguile*

Clo. Yea, forsooth, an your mistership be em-
    perial.   40

Tam. Empress I am, but yonder sits the emperor.

Clo. 'Tis he. God and Saint Stephen give you good
    den.

I have brought you a letter and a couple of pigeons
    here.

              He [Saturninus] reads the letter.

Sat. Go, take him away, and hang him presently. 44

Clo. How much money must I have?

Tam. Come, sirrah, you must be hanged.

    Clo. Hanged! By'r lady, then I have brought
up a neck to a fair end.   *Exit [guarded].* 48

Sat. Despiteful and intolerable wrongs!
Shall I endure this monstrous villainy?
I know from whence this same device proceeds:
May this be borne? As if his trait'rous sons,   52
That died by law for murther of our brother,
Have by my means been butcher'd wrongfully!
Go, drag the villain hither by the hair;
Nor age nor honour shall shape privilege.   56
For this proud mock I'll be thy slaughterman,
Sly frantic wretch, that holp'st to make me great,
In hope thyself should govern Rome and me.

           Enter Nuntius Æmilius.

What news with thee, Æmilius?   60

Æmil. Arm, my lords! Rome never had more cause.
The Goths have gather'd head, and with a power
Of high-resolved men, bent to the spoil,
They hither march amain, under conduct   64
Of Lucius, son to old Andronicus;

---

40 mistership: *the clown's attempt at 'mistress-ship'*
42 good den: *good evening*
56 shape privilege: *constitute exemption from punishment*

Who threats, in course of this revenge, to do
As much as ever Coriolanus did.

    Sat. Is warlike Lucius general of the Goths?   68
These tidings nip me, and I hang the head
As flowers with frost or grass beat down with storms.
Ay, now begins our sorrows to approach:
'Tis he the common people love so much.   72
Myself hath often heard them say,
When I have walked like a private man,
That Lucius' banishment was wrongfully,
And they have wish'd that Lucius were their em-
    peror.   76

    Tam. Why should you fear? is not your city strong?

    Sat. Ay, but the citizens favour Lucius,
And will revolt from me to succour him.

    Tam. King, be thy thoughts imperious, like thy
    name.   80
Is the sun dimm'd, that gnats do fly in it?
The eagle suffers little birds to sing,
And is not careful what they mean thereby,
Knowing that with the shadow of his wings   84
He can at pleasure stint their melody;
Even so mayst thou the giddy men of Rome.
Then cheer thy spirit; for know, thou emperor,
I will enchant the old Andronicus   88
With words more sweet, and yet more dangerous,
Than baits to fish, or honey-stalks to sheep,
Whenas the one is wounded with the bait,
The other rotted with delicious food.   92

    Sat. But he will not entreat his son for us.

    Tam. If Tamora entreat him, then he will:
For I can smooth and fill his aged ear

66 in course of: *in carrying out*   67 Coriolanus; *cf. n.*
71 begins: *begin*   85 stint: *stop*   90 honey-stalks; *cf. n.*
91 Whenas: *when*   95 smooth: *flatter*

With golden promises, that, were his heart   96
Almost impregnable, his old ears deaf,
Yet should both ear and heart obey my tongue.
[*To Æmilius.*] Go thou before, be our ambassador:
Say that the emperor requests a parley   100
Of warlike Lucius, and appoint the meeting,
Even at his father's house, the old Andronicus.
   Sat. Æmilius, do this message honourably:
And if he stand on hostage for his safety,   104
Bid him demand what pledge will please him best.
   Æmil. Your bidding shall I do effectually.   *Exit.*
   Tam. Now will I to that old Andronicus,
And temper him with all the art I have,   108
To pluck proud Lucius from the warlike Goths.
And now, sweet emperor, be blithe again,
And bury all thy fear in my devices.
   Sat. Then go successantly, and plead to him.   112
                               Exeunt.

ACT FIFTH

Scene One

[*Plains near Rome*]

Flourish.   Enter Lucius with an Army of Goths, with drum and colours.

   Luc. Approved warriors, and my faithful friends,
I have received letters from great Rome,
Which signify what hate they bear their emperor,
And how desirous of our sight they are.   4
Therefore, great lords, be, as your titles witness,
Imperious and impatient of your wrongs;

104 stand on hostage: *demand hostages*   108 temper: *influence*
112 successantly: *in succession* (?)   1 Approved: *tried*

And wherein Rome hath done you any scath,

Let him make treble satisfaction.   8

    [*1.*] *Goth.* Brave slip, sprung from the great An-
      dronicus,

Whose name was once our terror, now our comfort;

Whose high exploits and honourable deeds

Ingrateful Rome requites with foul contempt;   12

Be bold in us: we'll follow where thou lead'st,

Like stinging bees in hottest summer's day

Led by their master to the flower'd fields,

And be aveng'd on cursed Tamora.   16

    [*All the Goths.*] And, as he saith, so say we all with
    him.

    Luc. I humbly thank him, and I thank you all.

But who comes here, led by a lusty Goth?

*Enter a Goth, leading of Aaron, with his Child in his
        arms.*

    [*2.*] *Goth.* Renowned Lucius, from our troops I
    stray'd,   20

To gaze upon a ruinous monastery;

And as I earnestly did fix mine eye

Upon the wasted building, suddenly

I heard a child cry underneath a wall.   24

I made unto the noise; when soon I heard

The crying babe controll'd with this discourse:

'Peace, tawny slave, half me and half thy dam!

Did not thy hue bewray whose brat thou art,   28

Had nature lent thee but thy mother's look,

Villain, thou mightst have been an emperor:

But where the bull and cow are both milk-white,

They never do beget a coal-black calf.   32

Peace, villain, peace!'—even thus he rates the babe—

7 scath: *harm*   9 slip: *scion*
26 controll'd: *restrained*   33 rates: *scolds*

'For I must bear thee to a trusty Goth;
Who, when he knows thou art the empress' babe,
Will hold thee dearly for thy mother's sake.'   36
With this, my weapon drawn, I rush'd upon him,
Surpris'd him suddenly, and brought him hither,
To use as you think needful of the man.

  Luc. O worthy Goth, this is the incarnate devil   40
That robb'd Andronicus of his good hand:
This is the pearl that pleas'd your empress' eye,
And here's the base fruit of his burning lust.
Say, wall-ey'd slave, whither wouldst thou convey   44
This growing image of thy fiend-like face?
Why dost not speak? What! deaf? not a word?
A halter, soldiers! hang him on this tree,
And by his side his fruit of bastardy.   48

  Aar. Touch not the boy; he is of royal blood.

  Luc. Too like the sire for ever being good.
First hang the child, that he may see it sprawl;
A sight to vex the father's soul withal.   52
Get me a ladder.

                 [*A ladder is brought, which Aaron
                       is made to ascend.*]

  Aar.   Lucius, save the child;
And bear it from me to the empress.
If thou do this, I'll show thee wondrous things,
That highly may advantage thee to hear: 56
If thou wilt not, befall what may befall,
I'll speak no more but 'Vengeance rot you all!'

  Luc. Say on; and if it please me which thou
     speak'st,
Thy child shall live, and I will see it nourish'd.   60

  Aar. And if it please thee! why, assure thee, Lucius,

---

42 pearl . . . eye; *cf. n.*   44 wall-ey'd: *white-eyed*
50 for ever being: *ever to be*

'Twill vex thy soul to hear what I shall speak;
For I must talk of murthers, rapes, and massacres,
Acts of black night, abominable deeds,   64
Complots of mischief, treason, villainies
Ruthful to hear, yet piteously perform'd:
And this shall all be buried by my death,
Unless thou swear to me my child shall live.   68

   Luc. Tell on thy mind: I say, thy child shall live.

   Aar. Swear that he shall, and then I will begin.

   Luc. Who should I swear by? thou believ'st no god:
That granted, how canst thou believe an oath?   72

   Aar. What if I do not? as, indeed, I do not;
Yet, for I know thou art religious,
And hast a thing within thee called conscience,
With twenty popish tricks and ceremonies,   76
Which I have seen thee careful to observe,
Therefore I urge thy oath; for that I know
An idiot holds his bauble for a god,
And keeps the oath which by that god he swears,   80
To that I'll urge him: therefore thou shalt vow
By that same god, what god soe'er it be,
That thou ador'st and hast in reverence,
To save my boy, to nourish and bring him up: 84
Or else I will discover nought to thee.

   Luc. Even by my god I swear to thee I will.

   Aar. First, know thou, I begot him on the empress.

   Luc. O most insatiate, luxurious woman!   88

   Aar. Tut! Lucius, this was but a deed of charity
To that which thou shalt hear of me anon.
'Twas her two sons that murder'd Bassianus;
They cut thy sister's tongue and ravish'd her,   92
And cut her hands and trimm'd her as thou saw'st.

---

66 piteously: *pitiably*   74 for: *because*
78 urge: *insist upon*   79 idiot . . . bauble; *cf. n.*
88 luxurious: *lustful*

 Luc. O detestable villain! call'st thou that trim-
  ming?

 Aar. Why, she was wash'd, and cut, and trimm'd,
  and 'twas

Trim sport for them that had the doing of it. 96

 Luc. O barbarous, beastly villains, like thyself!

 Aar. Indeed, I was their tutor to instruct them.

That codding spirit had they from their mother,

As sure a card as ever won the set; 100

That bloody mind, I think, they learn'd of me,

As true a dog as ever fought at head.

Well, let my deeds be witness of my worth.

I train'd thy brethren to that guileful hole 104

Where the dead corpse of Bassianus lay;

I wrote the letter that thy father found,

And hid the gold within the letter mention'd,

Confederate with the queen and her two sons: 108

And what not done, that thou hast cause to rue,

Wherein I had no stroke of mischief in it?

I play'd the cheater for thy father's hand,

And, when I had it, drew myself apart, 112

And almost broke my heart with extreme laughter.

I pry'd me through the crevice of a wall

When, for his hand, he had his two sons' heads;

Beheld his tears, and laugh'd so heartily, 116

That both mine eyes were rainy like to his:

And when I told the empress of this sport,

She sounded almost at my pleasing tale,

And for my tidings gave me twenty kisses. 120

 [*1.*] *Goth.* What! canst thou say all this, and never
  blush?

 Aar. Ay, like a black dog, as the saying is.

---

99 codding: *lecherous*   104 train'd: *enticed*
109 what not done: *what was not done* 119 sounded: *swooned*
122 like a black dog; *cf. n.*

Luc. Art thou not sorry for these heinous deeds?

Aar. Ay, that I had not done a thousand more.   124
Even now I curse the day, and yet, I think,
Few come within the compass of my curse,
Wherein I did not some notorious ill:
As kill a man, or else devise his death;   128
Ravish a maid, or plot the way to do it;
Accuse some innocent, and forswear myself;
Set deadly enmity between two friends;
Make poor men's cattle break their necks;   132
Set fire on barns and hay-stacks in the night,
And bid the owners quench them with their tears.
Oft have I digg'd up dead men from their graves,
And set them upright at their dear friends' doors,   136
Even when their sorrows almost were forgot;
And on their skins, as on the bark of trees,
Have with my knife carved in Roman letters,
'Let not your sorrow die, though I am dead.'   140
Tut! I have done a thousand dreadful things
As willingly as one would kill a fly,
And nothing grieves me heartily indeed
But that I cannot do ten thousand more.   144

Luc. Bring down the devil, for he must not die
So sweet a death as hanging presently.

Aar. If there be devils, would I were a devil,
To live and burn in everlasting fire,   148
So I might have your company in hell,
But to torment you with my bitter tongue!

Luc. Sirs, stop his mouth, and let him speak no
     more.

[*Enter a Goth.*]

Goth. My lord, there is a messenger from Rome   152

124 ff. *Cf. n.*   145 Bring down the devil; *cf. n.*

Desires to be admitted to your presence.
   Luc. Let him come near.

Enter Æmilius.

Welcome, Æmilius! what's the news from Rome?
   Æmil. Lord Lucius, and you princes of the
      Goths,   156
The Roman emperor greets you all by me;
And, for he understands you are in arms,
He craves a parley at your father's house,
Willing you to demand your hostages,   160
And they shall be immediately deliver'd.
   [*1.*] *Goth.* What says our general?
   Luc. Æmilius, let the emperor give his pledges
Unto my father and my uncle Marcus,   164
And we will come.   March away.

Flourish.   Exeunt.

Scene Two

[*Rome.   Before Titus's House*]

Enter Tamora and her two Sons, disguised.

   Tam. Thus, in this strange and sad habiliment,
I will encounter with Andronicus,
And say I am Revenge, sent from below
To join with him and right his heinous wrongs.   4
Knock at his study, where, they say, he keeps,
To ruminate strange plots of dire revenge;
Tell him, Revenge is come to join with him,
And work confusion on his enemies.   8

They knock.   Titus opens his study door [*above*].
   Tit. Who doth molest my contemplation?

160 Willing: *desiring*   2 encounter with: *meet*

Is it your trick to make me ope the door,
That so my sad decrees may fly away,
And all my study be to no effect?   12
You are deceiv'd; for what I mean to do,
See here, in bloody lines I have set down;
And what is written shall be executed.

   Tam. Titus, I am come to talk with thee.   16

   Tit. No, not a word; how can I grace my talk,
Wanting a hand to give it action?
Thou hast the odds of me; therefore no more.

   Tam. If thou didst know me, thou wouldst talk with
     me.   20

   Tit. I am not mad; I know thee well enough:
Witness this wretched stump, witness these crimson
     lines;
Witness these trenches made by grief and care;
Witness the tiring day and heavy night;   24
Witness all sorrow, that I know thee well
For our proud empress, mighty Tamora.
Is not thy coming for my other hand?

   Tam. Know, thou sad man, I am not Tamora;   28
She is thy enemy, and I thy friend:
I am Revenge, sent from th' infernal kingdom,
To ease the gnawing vulture of thy mind,
By working wreakful vengeance on thy foes.   32
Come down, and welcome me to this world's light;
Confer with me of murder and of death.
There's not a hollow cave or lurking-place,
No vast obscurity or misty vale,   36
Where bloody murther or detested rape
Can couch for fear, but I will find them out;
And in their ears tell them my dreadful name,

11 sad decrees: *serious resolutions*   32 wreakful: *wrathful*
36 obscurity: *obscure place*

Revenge, which makes the foul offenders quake.   40
   Tit. Art thou Revenge? and art thou sent to me,
To be a torment to mine enemies?
   Tam. I am; therefore come down, and welcome me.
   Tit. Do me some service ere I come to thee.   44
Lo, by thy side where Rape and Murder stands;
Now give some surance that thou art Revenge:
Stab them, or tear them on thy chariot-wheels,
And then I'll come and be thy waggoner,   48
And whirl along with thee about the globes.
Provide thee two proper palfreys, black as jet,
To hale thy vengeful waggon swift away,
And find out murtherers in their guilty caves: 52
And when thy car is loaden with their heads,
I will dismount, and by the waggon-wheel
Trot like a servile footman all day long,
Even from Hyperion's rising in the east   56
Until his very downfall in the sea:
And day by day I'll do this heavy task,
So thou destroy Rapine and Murder there.
   Tam. These are my ministers, and come with me.   60
   Tit. Are these thy ministers? what are they call'd?
   Tam. Rape and Murder; therefore called so,
'Cause they take vengeance of such kind of men.
   Tit. Good Lord, how like the empress' sons they
      are,   64
And you the empress! but we worldly men
Have miserable, mad, mistaking eyes.
O sweet Revenge! now do I come to thee;
And, if one arm's embracement will content thee,   68
I will embrace thee in it by and by.   [*Exit above.*]
   Tam. This closing with him fits his lunacy.

46 surance: *assurance*   56 Hyperion: *the old sun-god*
59 Rapine: *rape*   65 worldly: *living in the world*
70 closing: *agreeing*

Whate'er I forge to feed his brain-sick fits,
Do you uphold and maintain in your speeches,   72
For now he firmly takes me for Revenge;
And, being credulous in this mad thought,
I'll make him send for Lucius his son;
And, whilst I at a banquet hold him sure,   76
I'll find some cunning practice out of hand
To scatter and disperse the giddy Goths,
Or, at the least, make them his enemies.
See, here he comes, and I must ply my theme.   80

[Enter Titus, below.]

Tit. Long have I been forlorn, and all for thee:
Welcome, dread Fury, to my woeful house:
Rapine and Murther, you are welcome too.
How like the empress and her sons you are!   84
Well are you fitted had you but a Moor:
Could not all hell afford you such a devil?
For well I wot the empress never wags
But in her company there is a Moor;   88
And would you represent our queen aright,
It were convenient you had such a devil.
But welcome, as you are.   What shall we do?

   Tam. What wouldst thou have us do, Andronicus? 92
   Dem. Show me a murtherer, I'll deal with him.
   Chi. Show me a villain that hath done a rape,
And I am sent to be reveng'd on him.

   Tam. Show me a thousand that have done thee
      wrong,   96
And I will be revenged on them all.

   Tit. Look round about the wicked streets of Rome,
And when thou find'st a man that's like thyself,
Good Murder, stab him; he's a murtherer.   100

77 practice: *stratagem*

Go thou with him; and when it is thy hap
To find another that is like to thee,
Good Rapine, stab him; he's a ravisher.
Go thou with them; and in the emperor's court   104
There is a queen attended by a Moor;
Well mayst thou know her by thy own proportion,
For up and down she doth resemble thee:
I pray thee, do on them some violent death;   108
They have been violent to me and mine.
    Tam. Well hast thou lesson'd us; this shall we do.
But would it please thee, good Andronicus,
To send for Lucius, thy thrice-valiant son,   112
Who leads towards Rome a band of warlike Goths,
And bid him come and banquet at thy house:
When he is here, even at thy solemn feast,
I will bring in the empress and her sons,   116
The emperor himself, and all thy foes,
And at thy mercy shall they stoop and kneel,
And on them shalt thou ease thy angry heart.
What says Andronicus to this device?   120
    Tit. Marcus, my brother! 'tis sad Titus calls.

Enter Marcus.

Go, gentle Marcus, to thy nephew Lucius;
Thou shalt inquire him out among the Goths:
Bid him repair to me, and bring with him   124
Some of the chiefest princes of the Goths;
Bid him encamp his soldiers where they are:
Tell him, the emperor and the empress too
Feast at my house, and he shall feast with them.   128
This do thou for my love; and so let him,
As he regards his aged father's life.
    Mar. This will I do, and soon return again. [*Exit.*]

107 up and down: *completely*

Tam. Now will I hence about thy business,   132
And take my ministers along with me.

Tit. Nay, nay, let Rape and Murder stay with me;
Or else I'll call my brother back again,
And cleave to no revenge but Lucius.   136

Tam. [*Aside to her sons.*] What say you, boys? will
        you bide with him,
Whiles I go tell my lord the emperor
How I have govern'd our determin'd jest?
Yield to his humour, smooth, and speak him fair,   140
And tarry with him till I turn again.

Tit. [*Aside.*] I know them all, though they suppose
        me mad;
And will o'erreach them in their own devices:
A pair of cursed hell-hounds and their dam.   144

Dem. [*Aside to Tamora.*] Madam, depart at pleas-
        ure; leave us here.

Tam. Farewell, Andronicus: Revenge now goes
To lay a complot to betray thy foes.   [*Exit Tamora.*]

Tit. I know thou dost; and, sweet Revenge, fare-
        well.   148

Chi. Tell us, old man, how shall we be employ'd?

Tit. Tut! I have work enough for you to do.
Publius, come hither, Caius and Valentine!

[*Enter Publius and Others.*]

Pub. What is your will?   152

Tit. Know you these two?

Pub. The empress' sons,
I take them, Chiron [and] Demetrius.

Tit. Fie, Publius, fie! thou art too much deceiv'd; 156
The one is Murder, Rape is the other's name;
And therefore bind them, gentle Publius;

139 govern'd . . . jest: *managed our proposed deception*
141 turn: *return*

Caius and Valentine, lay hands on them;
Oft have you heard me wish for such an hour,   160
And now I find it: therefore bind them sure,
[And stop their mouths, if they begin to cry.]

> [*Exit. Publius and the Others lay
> hold on Chiron and Demetrius.*]

  Chi. Villains, forbear! we are the empress' sons.
  Pub. And therefore do we what we are commanded.   164
Stop close their mouths, let them not speak a word.
Is he sure bound? look that you bind them fast.

*Enter Titus Andronicus with a knife, and Lavinia
with a basin.*

  Tit. Come, come, Lavinia; look, thy foes are bound.
Sirs, stop their mouths, let them not speak to me, 168
But let them hear what fearful words I utter.
O villains, Chiron and Demetrius!
Here stands the spring whom you have stain'd with
    mud,
This goodly summer with your winter mix'd.   172
You kill'd her husband, and for that vile fault
Two of her brothers were condemn'd to death,
My hand cut off and made a merry jest:
Both her sweet hands, her tongue, and that more
    dear   176
Than hands or tongue, her spotless chastity,
Inhuman traitors, you constrain'd and forc'd.
What would you say if I should let you speak?
Villains! for shame you could not beg for grace.   180
Hark, wretches! how I mean to martyr you.
This one hand yet is left to cut your throats,
Whilst that Lavinia 'tween her stumps doth hold
The basin that receives your guilty blood.   184

You know your mother means to feast with me,
And calls herself Revenge, and thinks me mad.
Hark! villains, I will grind your bones to dust,
And with your blood and it I'll make a paste;   188
And of the paste a coffin I will rear,
And make two pasties of your shameful heads;
And bid that strumpet, your unhallow'd dam,
Like to the earth swallow her own increase.   192
This is the feast that I have bid her to,
And this the banquet she shall surfeit on;
For worse than Philomel you us'd my daughter,
And worse than Progne I will be reveng'd.   196
And now prepare your throats. Lavinia, come.
Receive the blood: and when that they are dead,
Let me go grind their bones to powder small,
And with this hateful liquor temper it;   200
And in that paste let their vile heads be bak'd.
Come, come, be every one officious
To make this banquet, which I wish might prove
More stern and bloody than the Centaurs' feast.   204
          He cuts their throats.
So, now bring them in, for I'll play the cook,
And see them ready 'gainst their mother comes.
        Exeunt [bearing the dead bodies].

189 coffin: *pie-crust; cf. n.*
196 worse than Progne; *cf. n.*
202 officious: *active*

192 increase: *offspring*
200 temper: *mix*
204 Centaurs' feast; *cf. n.*

Scene Three

[*The Same.   The Court of Titus's House*]

*Enter Lucius, Marcus, and the Goths [with Aaron
prisoner].*

Luc. Uncle Marcus, since 'tis my father's mind
That I repair to Rome, I am content.
   [*1.*] *Goth.* And ours with thine, befall what fortune
      will.
   Luc. Good uncle, take you in this barbarous Moor, 4
This ravenous tiger, this accursed devil;
Let him receive no sustenance, fetter him,
Till he be brought unto the empress' face,
For testimony of her foul proceedings: 8
And see the ambush of our friends be strong;
I fear the emperor means no good to us.
   Aar. Some devil whisper curses in my ear,
And prompt me, that my tongue may utter forth   12
The venomous malice of my swelling heart!
   Luc. Away, inhuman dog! unhallow'd slave!
Sirs, help our uncle to convey him in.
                    [*Exeunt Goths, with Aaron.*] *Flourish*
                                          [*within*].
The trumpets show the emperor is at hand.   16

*Sound trumpets.   Enter Emperor and Empress, with
[Æmilius,] Tribunes, [Senators,] and Others.*

   Sat. What! hath the firmament more suns than one?
   Luc. What boots it thee, to call thyself a sun?
   Mar. Rome's emperor, and nephew, break the parle;
These quarrels must be quietly debated.   20
The feast is ready which the careful Titus

3 ours with thine: *our will is one with thine*
19 break the parle: *stop the parley*

Hath ordain'd to an honourable end,

For peace, for love, for league, and good to Rome:

Please you, therefore, draw nigh, and take your
    places.   24

    Sat. Marcus, we will.   *Hautboys.*

A table brought in. [*The Company sit down at
    table.*]   *Enter Titus, like a Cook, placing the
    meat on the table; and Lavinia with a veil over
    her face* [*and young Lucius with Others*].

    Tit. Welcome, my gracious lord; welcome, dread
    queen;

Welcome, ye warlike Goths; welcome, Lucius;

And welcome, all. Although the cheer be poor,   28

'Twill fill your stomachs, please you eat of it.

    Sat. Why art thou thus attir'd, Andronicus?

    Tit. Because I would be sure to have all well

To entertain your highness, and your empress.   32

    Tam. We are beholding to you, good Andronicus.

    Tit. An if your highness knew my heart, you were.

My lord the emperor, resolve me this:

Was it well done of rash Virginius   36

To slay his daughter with his own right hand,

Because she was enforc'd, stain'd, and deflower'd?

    Sat. It was, Andronicus.

    Tit. Your reason, mighty lord?   40

    Sat. Because the girl should not survive her shame,

And by her presence still renew his sorrows.

    Tit. A reason mighty, strong, and effectual;

A pattern, precedent, and lively warrant,   44

For me most wretched, to perform the like.

Die, die, Lavinia, and thy shame with thee;

33 beholding: *beholden*   35 resolve me: *tell me*
36, 37 rash Virginius . . . his daughter; *cf. n.*
38 enforc'd: *violated*

And with thy shame thy father's sorrow die!

> *He kills her.*

  Sat. What hast done, unnatural and unkind?   48
  Tit. Kill'd her, for whom my tears have made me
blind.

I am as woeful as Virginius was,

And have a thousand times more cause than he

[To do this outrage: and it now is done.]   52

  Sat. What! was she ravish'd? tell who did the deed.
  Tit. Will 't please you eat? will 't please your high-
ness feed?
  Tam. Why hast thou slain thine only daughter thus?
  Tit. Not I; 'twas Chiron and Demetrius: 56

They ravish'd her, and cut away her tongue:

And they, 'twas they, that did her all this wrong.

  Sat. Go fetch them hither to us presently.
  Tit. Why, there they are both, baked in that pie;   60

Whereof their mother daintily hath fed,

Eating the flesh that she herself hath bred.

'Tis true, 'tis true; witness my knife's sharp point.

> *He stabs the Empress.*

  Sat. Die, frantic wretch, for this accursed deed!   64

> [*Kills Titus.*]

  Luc. Can the son's eye behold his father bleed?

There's meed for meed, death for a deadly deed!

> [*Kills Saturninus. A great tumult. The
> people in confusion disperse. Mar-
> cus, Lucius, and their partisans go up
> into the balcony.*]

  Mar. You sad-fac'd men, people and sons of Rome,

By uproars sever'd, like a flight of fowl   68

Scatter'd by winds and high tempestuous gusts,

O! let me teach you how to knit again

66 meed for meed: *measure for measure*

This scatter'd corn into one mutual sheaf,
These broken limbs again into one body;   72
Lest Rome herself be bane unto herself,
And she whom mighty kingdoms curtsy to,
Like a forlorn and desperate castaway,
Do shameful execution on herself.   76
But if my frosty signs and chaps of age,
Grave witnesses of true experience,
Cannot induce you to attend my words,
[*To Lucius.*] Speak, Rome's dear friend, as erst our
    ancestor,   80
When with his solemn tongue he did discourse
To love-sick Dido's sad attending ear
The story of that baleful burning night
When subtle Greeks surpris'd King Priam's Troy;   84
Tell us what Sinon hath bewitch'd our ears,
Or who hath brought the fatal engine in
That gives our Troy, our Rome, the civil wound.
My heart is not compact of flint nor steel,   88
Nor can I utter all our bitter grief,
But floods of tears will drown my oratory,
And break my very utterance, even in the time
When it should move you to attend me most,   92
Lending your kind commiseration.
Here is a captain, let him tell the tale;
Your hearts will throb and weep to hear him speak.

  Luc. This, noble auditory, be it known to you,   96
That cursed Chiron and Demetrius
Were they that murdered our emperor's brother;
And they it was that ravished our sister.
For their fell faults our brothers were beheaded,   100

---

71 mutual: *united*   77 chaps: *wrinkles*
80 our ancestor: *Æneas*   85 Sinon; *cf. n.*
88 compact: *composed*   93-97 *Cf. n.*   100 fell: *cruel*

Our father's tears despis'd, and basely cozen'd
Of that true hand that fought Rome's quarrel out,
And sent her enemies unto the grave:
Lastly, myself unkindly banished,   104
The gates shut on me, and turn'd weeping out,
To beg relief among Rome's enemies;
Who drown'd their enmity in my true tears,
And op'd their arms to embrace me as a friend: 108
And I am turn'd forth, be it known to you,
That have preserv'd her welfare in my blood,
And from her bosom took the enemy's point,
Sheathing the steel in my adventurous body.   112
Alas! you know I am no vaunter, I;
My scars can witness, dumb although they are,
That my report is just and full of truth.
But, soft! methinks I do digress too much,   116
Citing my worthless praise: O, pardon me!
For when no friends are by, men praise themselves.
    Mar. Now is my turn to speak. Behold this child;
                          [*Pointing to the Child in the arms
                                   of an Attendant.*]
Of this was Tamora delivered,   120
The issue of an irreligious Moor,
Chief architect and plotter of these woes.
The villain is alive in Titus' house,
Damn'd as he is, to witness this is true.   124
Now judge what cause had Titus to revenge
These wrongs, unspeakable, past patience,
Or more than any living man could bear.
Now you have heard the truth, what say you Ro-
    mans?   128
Have we done aught amiss, show us wherein,

---

101 and basely cozen'd: *and* [*he*] *basely cheated*
124 Damn'd as he is; *cf. n.*

And, from the place where you behold us now,
The poor remainder of Andronici
Will, hand in hand, all headlong cast us down,   132
And on the ragged stones beat forth our brains,
And make a mutual closure of our house.
Speak, Romans, speak! and if you say we shall,
Lo! hand in hand, Lucius and I will fall.   136
    Æmil. Come, come, thou reverend man of Rome,
And bring our emperor gently in thy hand,
Lucius, our emperor; for well I know
The common voice do cry it shall be so.   140
    [*Romans.*] Lucius, all hail! Rome's royal emperor!
    Mar. [*To Attendants.*] Go, go into old Titus' sor-
            rowful house,
And hither hale that misbelieving Moor,
To be adjudg'd some direful slaughtering death,   144
As punishment for his most wicked life.
                            [*Exeunt Attendants.*]
            [*Lucius, Marcus, and the Others descend.*]
    [*Romans.*] Lucius, all hail! Rome's gracious gover-
            nor!
    Luc. Thanks, gentle Romans: may I govern so,
To heal Rome's harms, and wipe away her woe!   148
But, gentle people, give me aim awhile,
For nature puts me to a heavy task.
Stand all aloof; but, uncle, draw you near,
To shed obsequious tears upon this trunk.   152
O! take this warm kiss on thy pale cold lips,
                            [*Kisses Titus.*]
These sorrowful drops upon thy blood-stain'd face,
The last true duties of thy noble son!
    Mar. Tear for tear, and loving kiss for kiss,   156

134 closure: *end*   149 give me aim; *cf. n.*
152 obsequious tears: *tears befitting a funeral*

Thy brother Marcus tenders on thy lips:
O! were the sum of these that I should pay
Countless and infinite, yet would I pay them.

   Luc. Come hither, boy; come, come, and learn of
    us   160
To melt in showers: thy grandsire lov'd thee well:
Many a time he danc'd thee on his knee,
Sung thee asleep, his loving breast thy pillow;
Many a matter hath he told to thee,   164
Meet and agreeing with thine infancy;
In that respect, then, like a loving child,
Shed yet some small drops from thy tender spring,
Because kind nature doth require it so: 168
Friends should associate friends in grief and woe.
Bid him farewell; commit him to the grave;
Do him that kindness, and take leave of him.

   Boy. O grandsire, grandsire! even with all my
    heart   172
Would I were dead, so you did live again.
O Lord! I cannot speak to him for weeping;
My tears will choke me if I ope my mouth.

      [Re-enter Attendants with Aaron.]

   [1.] Roman. You sad Andronici, have done with
    woes: 176
Give sentence on this execrable wretch,
That hath been breeder of these dire events.

   Luc. Set him breast-deep in earth, and famish him;
There let him stand, and rave, and cry for food: 180
If any one relieves or pities him,
For the offence he dies. This is our doom:
Some stay to see him fasten'd in the earth.

165-169 *Cf. n.*   169 associate: *accompany*

Aar. O, why should wrath be mute, and fury
 dumb?   184
I am no baby, I, that with base prayers
I should repent the evils I have done.
Ten thousand worse than ever yet I did
Would I perform, if I might have my will: 188
If one good deed in all my life I did,
I do repent it from my very soul.
 Luc. Some loving friends convey the emperor hence,
And give him burial in his father's grave. 192
My father and Lavinia shall forthwith
Be closed in our household's monument.
As for that heinous tiger, Tamora,
No funeral rite, nor man in mournful weeds! 196
No mournful bell shall ring her burial;
But throw her forth to beasts and birds of prey.
Her life was beast-like, and devoid of pity;
And, being so, shall have like want of pity. 200
See justice done on Aaron, that damn'd Moor,
By whom our heavy haps had their beginning:
Then, afterwards, to order well the state,
That like events may ne'er it ruinate. 204

           Exeunt omnes.

200 *Cf. n.*

FINIS.

NOTES

Dramatis Personæ. A list of characters was first given in Rowe's edition of 1709. The First Folio divides the play into acts, of which the first is headed *Actus Primus. Scœna Prima.* There is no further division into scenes.

I. i. S. d. *aloft.* The tribunes and senators enter on the gallery which was situated at the back of the Elizabethan stage, and served a variety of purposes. It was, e.g., the balcony from which Juliet speaks to Romeo in *Romeo and Juliet,* and in *The Taming of the Shrew* it served as the gallery from which Christopher Sly and his attendants watch the play performed on the lower stage. Cf. also below, I. i. 298 and V. ii. 8.

I. i. 9. *Romans.* 'As a matter of orthoepy, it is perhaps worthy of notice that throughout this play, and generally in English books printed before the middle of the seventeenth century, this word is spelled *Romaines* or *Romanes.* "Romaine" could hardly have been pronounced *Roman.*' (White.)

I. i. 35. *In coffins from the field.* After these words in the Quarto of 1594, there is a passage of three and a half lines which was omitted from the later texts. Lines 35-38 in the 1594 Quarto read as follows:

'In coffins from the field, and at this day
To the Monument of that Andronicy
Done sacrifice of expiation
And slaine the Noblest prisoner of the Gothes.'

I. i. 64. Because of the fact that there is a distinct break here between the action that has just finished and that now commencing, Pope, Capell, Malone, and other editors begin a new scene with line 64. There is no change of place, however, and later editors prefer to make no change in the scene.

I. i. 98. *Ad manes fratrum sacrifice his flesh.* Human sacrifices to propitiate the shades of the dead were, of course, unknown in Rome, but neither the author nor his audience was scrupulous with respect to historical or geographical accuracy. Cf. note on I. i. 323.

I. i. 117-119. *Wilt thou draw near . . . nobility's true badge.* It is hardly necessary to mention the resemblance between this sentiment of Tamora's and that expressed by Portia, *Merchant of Venice,* IV. i. 184-202.

I. i. 131. *Was ever Scythia half so barbarous?* Cf. *King Lear,* I. i. 118-120:

> 'The barbarous Scythian
> Or he that makes his generation messes
> To gorge his appetite.'

I. i. 138. *the Thracian tyrant.* Polymnestor, upon whom Hecuba, Queen of Troy, took vengeance for the death of her son, Polydorus. It was not in *his* tent, however, but in her own, to which she had induced Polymnestor to come, that she made the 'opportunity of sharp revenge.' The allusion is to the *Hecuba* of Euripides, which had not been translated into English in Shakespeare's time.

I. i. 154. *grudges.* The Quarto of 1600 has *drugs,* but the Quarto of 1611 and the First Folio have *grudges,* a word which seems to be more in keeping with the sense of the preceding line.

I. i. 168. *fame's eternal date.* Cf. *Sonnets,* 18. 4:

'And summer's lease hath all too short a date.'

Dr. Johnson remarks: 'To *outlive an eternal date* is, though not philosophical, yet poetical sense. He wishes that her life may be longer than his, and her praise longer than fame.'

I. i. 177. *Solon's happiness.* Alluding to the remarks of the philosopher Solon to Crœsus, king of Lydia, to the effect that true happiness is dependent on honor, and that no man can be finally adjudged happy until after his death. Cf. *Herodotus*, 1. 32.

I. i. 217. *people's tribunes.* The First Folio has 'noble tribunes.' It may be that it was originally written 'people's,' and changed to 'noble' when the play was acted, as the latter word is somewhat more sonorous.

I. i. 312. *bandy.* A term from the game of tennis, meaning to strike the ball to and fro.

I. i. 323. *priest and holy water.* Such references to Christian ritual are, of course, anachronistic, but in the true Shakespearean manner. Cf. the 'popish tricks and ceremonies' of V. i. 76 below.

I. i. 379. *Ajax.* This seems to be an allusion to the *Ajax* of Sophocles, in which Ulysses pleads with Agamemnon for permission to bury the body of Ajax. So far as is known the *Ajax* had not been translated into English in Shakespeare's day.

I. i. 399. *you have play'd your prize.* Won what you were competing for. 'A metaphor borrowed from the fencing schools, prizes being played for certain degrees in the schools where the art of defence was taught—degrees of Master, Provost, and Scholar.' (Dyce's *Glossary*.)

I. i. 485. *Stand up.* These two words were regarded as stage directions by Pope and by several editors after him. In the quartos and folios, they form the first part of what in our text is line 486.

I. i. 491. *love-day.* A day appointed by the Church for the settlement of disputes amicably out of court, by an umpire. Cf. Gower, *Confessio Amantis*, I. 39.

> 'Hell is full of such discord
> That there may be no loveday.'

I. i. 493. *To hunt the panther.* The same type of imagination which infested the Roman forest with panthers introduced the lioness to the forest of Arden, and brought the bear to the seacoast of Bohemia and to the woods of Crete.

II. i. 14. *mount her pitch.* Pitch = point. A technical expression in falconry denoting the height to which a falcon soars before attacking the prey. Cf. Romeo's remarks, *Romeo and Juliet,* I. iv. 19 ff.

> 'I am too sore enpierced with his shaft,
> To soar with his light feathers; and so bound,
> I cannot bound a pitch above dull woe.'

Aaron means that he will soar to whatever height Tamora attains.

II. i. 17. *Prometheus tied to Caucasus.* No other play of Shakespeare's is so full of allusions to classical mythology, or contains so many Latin expressions and Latinized forms as *Titus Andronicus.*

II. i. 22. *Semiramis.* This legendary queen of Assyria was famous alike for her cruelty and her voluptuousness.

II. i. 37. *Clubs, clubs!* A call for men armed with clubs to put down a disturbance. It was a familiar cry in the streets of Elizabethan London. Originally the rallying cry of the apprentices, it became later the regular call for the policemen.

II. i. 41. *lath.* The stage sword or dagger used by the Vice in the old moralities was made of a lath, and the latter term came quite naturally to be used for an ineffective weapon. Cf. *Twelfth Night,* IV. ii. 138 ff.

II. i. 53. *Not I.* Warburton suggested that this speech be given to Chiron, and the following to Demetrius, on the not very plausible ground that it is Chiron who has made the 'reproachful speeches.'

II. i. 70. *This discord's ground.* 'There is a play upon the musical sense of *ground* (="plain-song" or theme).' (Rolfe.)

II. i. 82. *She is a woman, etc.* A quasi-proverbial expression found in several plays of Shakespeare, as well as elsewhere. Cf. *1 Henry VI*, V. iii. 78, 79:

> 'She's beautiful and therefore to be woo'd,
> She is a woman, therefore to be won.'

II. i. 85-87. *more water glideth by the mill, Than wots the miller of; and easy it is Of a cut loaf to steal a shive.* Collier noted the fact that both of these proverbs occur within a page of each other in *The Cobler of Canterburie,* 1590: 'Much water runnes by the mill that the miller wots not on. . . . The Prior perceived that the scull had cut a shive on his loafe.' (Cf. Ouvry's reprint, London, 1862, pp. 12 ff.) Both *The Cobler of Canterburie* and *Titus Andronicus* have been attributed to Greene. Cf. Appendix C. Rolfe quotes the Scottish proverb, 'Mickle water goes by the miller when he sleeps.'

II. i. 89. *Vulcan's badge.* The cuckold's horns. The allusion is to the intrigue of Mars and Venus, the wife of Vulcan.

II. i. 108. *Lucrece was not more chaste.* The story of Tarquin's rape of Lucrece seems to have been much in the mind of the author at this time. Cf. below IV. i. 63, 89 ff. Shakespeare's *Rape of Lucrece* was printed first in 1594, the date also of the first Quarto of *Titus Andronicus.* On the similarities between the two works, see Appendix C.

II. i. 120. *sacred wit.* Although sacred is usually taken here as a Latinism meaning *accursed,* there is, as has been noted in some quarters, an ironical sound about the word in this connection which accords well with Aaron's character.

II. i. 126. *house of Fame.* An obvious allusion to Chaucer's *Hous of Fame,* III. 291-300. A still earlier version, of course, is that of Vergil; cf. *Æneid,* IV. 183 ff.

II. i. 135. *Per Styga,* etc. The poet is apparently quoting from memory a line from Seneca, with whose tragedies he was undoubtedly familiar. In this connection, cf. Seneca's *Hippolytus,* 1180:

'Per Styga, per amnes igneos amens sequar,'

and *Hercules Furens,* 90, 91:

'Iam Styga et manes feros
Fugisse credis?'

II. ii. 1. *the morn is bright and grey.* Much pedantic discussion has taken place as to the precise meaning of the term grey, which Shakespeare uses constantly in describing the morning sky. But from the context here and elsewhere, there seems no reason for thinking that it means anything but bright, and that in the expression in our text, as in the other cases, it is not synonymous with the word bright. Cf. *Much Ado About Nothing,* V. iii. 25 ff.:

'the gentle day . . .
Dapples the drowsy east with spots of grey.'

By the same token, the *grey-ey'd* morn of *Romeo and Juliet,* II. iii. 1, is the *bright-eyed* morn.

II. ii. 3. *Uncouple here.* Loose the hounds. This passage with its reference to hunting and the joy of being in the open is strikingly suggestive of the descriptions of the hunt in *Venus and Adonis.* The latter was printed in 1593, one year before the publication of *Titus Andronicus,* and a date not so far removed from Shakespeare's own hunting days in Warwickshire. Cf. below, II. iii. 17-19.

II. ii. 9. *I have been troubled.* There is nothing more suggestive of the Shakespearean authorship of the play than these presentiments of evil, of which the poet constantly makes use in all his tragedies. Cf. below, II. iii. 195 ff.

II. iii. 9. *alms out of the empress' chest.* Rather obscure, but apparently meaning, as Stoll suggests, that Aaron has taken the gold from Tamora's chest.

II. iii. 17-19. *babbling echo mocks the hounds . . . a double hunt were heard at once.* Cf. the strikingly similar lines in *Venus and Adonis,* 695, 696:

'Then do they spend their mouths: Echo replies, As if another chase were in the skies.'

For other similarities between this play and *Venus and Adonis,* cf. Appendix C.

II. iii. 31. *Saturn is dominator.* According to the mediæval theory, persons born under the domination of the planet Saturn were of a morose, or *saturnine,* disposition. Collins quotes Greene, *Planetomachia,* 1585: 'The star of Saturn is especially cooling.' The planet Venus, which, according to Aaron, governs Tamora's disposition, has an entirely different influence.

II. iii. 43. *Philomel.* Philomela, daughter of Pandion, was ravished by Tereus, king of Thrace, who was the husband of her sister, Progne. Tereus then cut out her tongue to prevent her exposing him. That the story had made a deep impression on the poet's mind is witnessed by the frequent allusions to it in this play (cf. below, II. iv. 43, IV. i. 47 ff., and V. ii. 195). Cf. also in this connection the *Rape of Lucrece,* 1128-1134.

II. iii. 63. *With horns, as was Actæon's.* Actæon, a Theban prince, while hunting, accidentally saw Diana bathing, and was transformed by her into a stag, to be slain immediately by his dogs. The 'horns' which Tamora would fain see on Bassianus' temples are, of course, those of the cuckold.

II. iii. 72. *swarth Cimmerian.* Homer (cf. *Odyssey*, XI. 14) describes the Cimmerians as dwelling on the confines of the earth, 'shrouded in mist and darkness . . . and never does the shining sun look down on them.' Cf. Milton's 'dark Cimmerian desert' (*L'Allegro*, 10).

II. iii. 86. *these slips have made him noted long.* Dr. Johnson points out the fact that Tamora and Saturninus have presumably been married but one night.

II. iii. 93. *barren detested vale.* Tamora's description of this place here and in the lines immediately following is rather at variance with her description of it above (II. iii. 12-16). Or are we to assume that the scene has changed during the action?

II. iii. 110. *Lascivious Goth.* The Elizabethans pronounced *Goth* to sound like *goat*, and Shakespeare frequently quibbles on the word. Cf. *As You Like It*, III. iii. 7-9: 'I am here with thee and thy goats, as the most capricious poet, honest Ovid, was among the Goths.' (*Capricious* is from the Latin *capra*, goat.)

II. iii. 126. *And with that painted hope braves your mightiness.* The line stands thus in all the quartos and in the First Folio. The second, third, and fourth folios insert 'she' before 'braves.' It presents a crux as famous as any in Shakespeare. Various emendations have been suggested, and White suggests with reservations the reading, 'And with that faint hope braves, etc.' C. D. Stewart, in *Some Textual Difficulties in Shakespeare*, p. 156, offers the following interpretation: 'A painting occupies a position half way between the unsubstantial, uncertain, self-supported vision of a thing and the thing itself. Now when Lavinia gave him [Demetrius] such refusals his *hope* of success became more vivid. When she spoke of her chastity and gave excuses that were no real excuses to him, she only aggravated his passion and seemed to be artfully drawing him on; and only to refuse him. It was as if she had painted the picture of his success with her own hands, or in her own person, and held it up before him. She made herself a "painted hope." This is simply a hope whose pictures are more vivid, more real, than the uncertain visions of hope unassisted.'

II. iii. 151, 152. *The lion, mov'd with pity, did endure To have his princely paws par'd all away.* Probably an allusion to the story of Androclus and the lion.

II. iii. 153. *Some say that ravens foster forlorn children.* Doubtless a bit of folklore. Cf. *The Winter's Tale,* II. iii. 185, 186:

'Some powerful spirit instruct the kites and ravens
To be thy nurses.'

The Biblical story of the feeding of Elijah by ravens may have given rise to it. Cf. 1 Kings 17. 3-6.

II. iii. 227. *A precious ring, that lightens all the hole.* Probably an allusion to the carbuncle, formerly believed to emit radiance of its own in the dark.

II. iii. 231. *So pale did shine the moon on Pyramus.* Cf. *Midsummer Night's Dream,* III. i. 50 ff.

II. iv. 5. *See, how with signs and tokens she can scrowl.* Ironically enough, Demetrius here suggests the very means by which Lavinia later exposes his crime, thus inciting her father to kill him. Cf. *King Lear,* III. vii. 56, 57, where Gloucester unwittingly pictures to Regan, in speaking of her treatment of Lear, the torture which Cornwall and she are to inflict upon him immediately afterward.

II. iv. 26. *some Tereus hath deflower'd thee.* Cf. note on II. iii. 43.

II. iv. 39. *in a tedious sampler sew'd her mind.* Philomela, after being ravished and mutilated by Tereus, made known her condition by working a sampler on which she told the story.

II. iv. 51. *Cerberus at the Thracian poet's feet.*
Orpheus, when he descended into Hades to seek his
wife, Eurydice, was able by his music to charm Cerberus, the triple-headed watch-dog of the infernal
regions.

III. i. 10. *two-and-twenty sons.* Is Titus here including among the two-and-twenty who died 'in
honour's lofty bed' his son Mutius, whom he has slain
(cf. I. i. 291) for what he considered a dishonorable
deed? If not, he was the father of twenty-six sons
instead of the five-and-twenty of I. i. 79. Baildon
suggests (*Arden Shakespeare*) that 'Shakespeare had
invented the Mutius episode and forgotten to alter the
original number.'

III. i. 34-37. *They would not mark me . . . tell
my sorrows to the stones.* This passage as it stands in
the First Folio is manifestly corrupt, reading as
follows:

'if they did heare
They would not marke me: oh if they did heare
They would not pitty me.
Therefore I tell my sorrowes bootles to the stones.'

The reading in our text is from the Quarto of 1600,
and although perhaps slightly corrupt, seems the most
nearly satisfactory of the various readings.

III. i. 150. *limbo.* Popularly used for hell, but,
in the strict sense of the term, *limbo* is not hell or
any place of punishment, but, according to mediæval
theology, a region bordering hell, where dwelt the
patriarchs, who died before the resurrection of Christ.
They were believed to have been carried to heaven
with our Lord at his ascension. The souls of un-
baptized infants are, according to other theories, also
assigned to limbo.

III. i. 170. *Writing destruction on the enemy's
castle.* This line, as might be expected from the un-

usual expression, has caused much trouble to commentators. Nares explains the word castle as meaning a kind of helmet, quoting unconvincingly from *Troilus and Cressida* (V. ii. 184):

'Stand fast, and wear a castle on thy head.'

III. i. 244. *some deal*. Deal is from the *O. E. Dæl*, part. Cf. Chaucer, *Legend of Good Women*, 1182, 1183:

'Her suster Anne, as she that coude her good,
Seide as her thoughte, and somdel hit withstood.'

The word survives to-day in such expressions as *a good deal*, etc.

III. ii. This scene appears for the first time in the First Folio.

III. ii. 4. *sorrow-wreathen knot*. Marcus' arms, which are crossed on his breast in an attitude of profound grief. Cf. *The Tempest*, I. ii. 224, 'His arms in this sad knot.'

III. ii. 15. *Wound it with sighing, girl, kill it with groans*. It was formerly thought that a heavy sigh draws a drop of blood from the heart. Cf. *Midsummer Night's Dream*, III. ii. 96, 97:

'All fancy-sick she is and pale of cheer,
With sighs of love, that costs the fresh blood dear.'

III. ii. 38. *Brew'd with her sorrow, mash'd upon her cheeks*. A rather prosaic allusion to the mash-tub and the operations of the brewing-house.

IV. i. 20, 21. *Hecuba of Troy Ran mad through sorrow*. After avenging the death of her son, Polydorus, Hecuba, wife of Priam, ran mad. Cf. above, note on I. i. 138.

IV. i. 37. Immediately before this line in the Folio occur the words, 'What booke?' Most modern editors omit them from the text, concurring in Dyce's opinion that 'the transcriber had inadvertently passed on to the line, *Lucius, what book,* etc., and when he afterwards perceived his mistake, and drew his pen through the misplaced line, he may have left two words of it not fully blotted out.'

IV. i. 81, 82. *Magni dominator poli,* etc. Cf. Seneca's *Hippolytus,* 671, 672:

> 'Magne regnator deum,
> Tam lentus audis scelera? Tam lentus vides?'

The poet is probably trying to quote from memory, and gets his terms confused. Seneca's tragedies abound in such similar epithets as *regnator deum, dominator poli, gubernator poli,* etc.

IV. i. 87-91. *My lord, kneel down . . . Lord Junius Brutus sware for Lucrece' rape.* Cf. the very similar lines in the *Rape of Lucrece* (1846-1848):

> 'Then jointly to the ground their knees they bow;
> And that deep vow, which Brutus made before,
> He doth again repeat, and that they swore.'

IV. i. 105. *Sibyl's leaves.* The leaves of the prophetic books of the Cumæan Sibyl, a woman of oracular powers, who, in classical mythology, appeared before Tarquin the Proud, offering him her nine books for three hundred pieces of gold. He refused to buy them, whereupon she burned three of the books and then returned, offering the remaining six for the original price. Tarquin again refused. The Sibyl again burned three books, and returned with a final offer of the remaining three for the price of the original nine. Tarquin, advised by his augur, then paid the three hundred pieces of gold for the three books, and the Sibyl disappeared. In times of political trouble, the Romans used to consult the Sibylline books. Cf. *Æneid,* VI. 1-75.

IV. ii. 20, 21. *Integer vitæ,* etc. The beginning of the famous twenty-second ode of the first book of

Horace. 'He who is pure in life and unstained from
sin, needs not the darts of the Moor, nor the bow.'
Shakespeare is much more likely than Chiron to have
'read it in the grammar long ago.'

IV. ii. 26. *no sound jest.* 'No joking matter.'
The quartos have *found,* which Theobald considered a
misprint for *fond.*

IV. ii. 72. *'Zounds.* The oath, *'Zounds* ('God's
wounds'), which is found in all the quartos, is replaced
in the First Folio by the expression 'Out!' because of
the statute of 1606 forbidding swearing, blasphemy,
etc., on the stage.

IV. ii. 73. *blowse.* 'If "blowsy" mean ruddy and
fat-faced, which it seems to do, the substantive would
seem not correctly applied to a new-born black-a-moor
child. Perhaps it had passed into a familiar term of
jocose endearment for a child.' (White.)

IV. ii. 95. *Typhon's brood.* Typhon, or Typheus,
one of the Titans, who, with his brood, dwelt in the
infernal regions and waged war against Zeus and the
other Olympian gods.

IV. ii. 154. *Not far, one Muli lives.* Steevens was
the first to correct the reading of the old editions, 'Not
far, one Muliteus.'

IV. iii. 4. *Terras Astræa reliquit.* Cf. Ovid,
Metamorphoses, I. 150. Astræa, the goddess of justice, was the last of all the gods to forsake mankind.

IV. iii. 43, 44. *I'll dive into the burning lake
below, And pull her out of Acheron by the heels.*
Acheron, the river of woe in Hades, is here referred
to as a burning lake, doubtless by confusion with the
Christian lake of fire and brimstone. Titus' rant
reminds the reader at once of Hotspur's intention (*1
Henry IV,* I. iii. 203 ff.) to

> 'dive into the bottom of the deep, . . .
> And pluck up drowned honour by the locks.'

IV. iii. 64-70. *Virgo . . . Taurus . . . Aries.*

The constellation *Virgo* (the Virgin) was supposed to represent Astræa after she had left the earth (cf. IV. iii. 4). *Taurus* (the Bull) and *Aries* (the Ram) are also zodiacal constellations.

IV. iv. 67. *Coriolanus.* This is the theme of Shakespeare's last tragedy, *Coriolanus,* which was written about 1608 or 1609.

IV. iv. 90. *honey-stalks.* According to Dr. Johnson, honey-stalks are sweet-clover flowers.

V. i. 42. *the pearl that pleas'd your empress' eye.* Alluding to an old proverb, which Shakespeare uses in *Two Gentlemen of Verona* (V. ii. 11, 12),

> 'the old saying is,
> Black men are pearls in beauteous ladies' eyes.'

V. i. 79. *An idiot holds his bauble for a god.* The bauble was the carved head with asses' ears that surmounted the baton which was carried by the court fool as a mock emblem of his office.

V. i. 122. *like a black dog, as the saying is.* 'To blush like a black dog' is one of the old proverbs in Ray's collection.

V. i. 124 ff. Aaron's circumstantial account of his misdeeds suggests at once the similar list of offences for which Barabas claims credit in Marlowe's *Jew of Malta* (II. iii. 177 ff.).

V. i. 145. *Bring down the devil.* Aaron's speech has evidently just been made from the top of the ladder on which he was to be hanged.

V. ii. 189. *of the paste a coffin I will rear.* In early English cookery books the crust of a pie was always known as the coffin. According to Selden (cf. *Table-Talk,* under *Christmas*), Christmas pies were baked originally in a long coffin-shaped crust, in imitation of the manger in which our Lord was laid at his birth.

V. ii. 196. *worse than Progne I will be reveng'd.*

The author's absorbing interest in the story of the ravishment and mutilation of Philomela by Tereus has been mentioned (cf. note on II. iii. 43). After Tereus had cut out her tongue, Philomela embroidered the story of her wrongs on a sampler, which she sent to her sister, Progne, wife of Tereus. The two sisters then revenged themselves on the guilty husband by murdering his son, Itylus, and serving his body at a banquet to his father. As a result of the horrible affair, Philomela was changed into a nightingale, Progne into a swallow, and Tereus into a hawk.

V. ii. 204. *the Centaurs' feast.* A reference to the story in classical mythology (told by Ovid in the twelfth book of the *Metamorphoses*) of the battle between the Centaurs and the Lapithæ, at the wedding-feast of Hippodamia and Pirithous. Cf. *Midsummer Night's Dream,* V. i. 44.

V. iii. 36-38. *Was it well done of rash Virginius To slay his daughter . . . stain'd and deflower'd?* In 449 B.C., Virginius, a centurion, slew his daughter, Virginia, to save her from Appius Claudius, the decemvir, who had attempted to violate her. The story was a favorite with the Elizabethans, and a drama on the subject, *The Tragicall Comedie of Apius and Virginia,* appeared about 1563. See Macaulay's *Lays of Ancient Rome.* The story is incorrectly given in the text.

V. iii. 85. *Sinon.* The Greek who persuaded the Trojans to admit the wooden horse into Troy.

V. iii. 93-97. In the 1594 Quarto these lines read as follows:

'And force you to commiseration,
Here's Rome's young captain, let him tell the tale,
While I stand by and weep to hear him speak.
   Lucius. Then, gracious auditory, be it known to you,
That Chiron and the damn'd Demetrius,' etc.

V. iii. 124. *Damn'd as he is.* The quartos and folios have *And as he is,* which Theobald emended to the reading given in the text. Cf. Brabantio's remark (*Othello,* I. ii. 63),

'Damn'd as thou art, thou hast enchanted her.'

V. iii. 149. *give me aim awhile.* Stand by and observe the result of my efforts. A figure from archery. The person who 'gave aim' stood near the target and reported the success of the shots. White suggests, 'Give me air awhile.' Schmidt, retaining the original reading, paraphrases, 'Give room and scope to my thoughts.'

V. iii. 165-169. These lines appear for the first time in the Quarto of 1600. In their place, the Quarto of 1594 has the following five lines:

'And bid thee bear his pretty tales in mind,
And talk of them when he was dead and gone.
    Mar. How many thousand times hath these poor
        lips,
When they were living, warmed themselves on thine!
O now, sweet boy, give them their latest kiss;' etc.

V. iii. 200. In the Quarto of 1594 this line reads,

'And being dead let birds on her take pity.'

APPENDIX A

Sources of the Play

No single and direct source of the story of *Titus Andronicus* has ever been discovered. It is probable that the play as we have it was based on an older play, but there is no conclusive evidence of the existence of any version, English or foreign, prior to the text that we now have. The plot seems, however, to combine many themes and incidents found in other forms of literature. The story proper is apparently without any historical basis, and is curiously anachronistic in arrangement. A Roman emperor and a tribune are made contemporary; the emperor is engaged, as no Roman emperor ever was, in warring upon the Goths; and the Rome in which the scene is laid is, according to Aaron the Moor, the seat of 'Popish ceremonies.' As for the surname, Andronicus, no Roman emperor ever bore it, although there was a Byzantine emperor, Andronicus Comnenus, of the twelfth century A.D., and it is not without significance that he is represented by Nicetas Choniata as having shot arrows with certain devices attached in the siege of Prusa. It may be worth noting, too, that after the removal of the empire to Byzantium in the fourth century there were wars with the Goths, and thus a remote historical background for some of the incidents of the play may be postulated. Finally, the similarity of the name Tamora to that of Tomyris, the vengeful queen of the Getæ, has been pointed out.

Baildon (Arden ed.) suggests an Oriental origin for the story, in view of its peculiar cruelty and lavish bloodshed, and the presence in it of those two Bashi-bazouks, Chiron and Demetrius. But if the story came from the Orient, it has undergone many modifications in transit.

The different threads of the plot of *Titus Andronicus* bear striking resemblance to other well-known themes and legends. The author frequently likens Lavinia's fate to that of Philomela, which Ovid's *Metamorphoses* had made known to England. The cruelty and villainy of Aaron suggest at once the deeds of Barabas and Ithamore in Marlowe's *Jew of Malta.* There is, furthermore, in Evans's *Old Ballads* and in the *Roxburghe Ballads,* a poem of about 1570 entitled, '*A Lamentable Ballad of the Tragical End of a Gallant Lord and of his Beautiful Lady, with the untimely death of their children, wickedly performed by a heathen Blackamore, their servant: The like seldom heard before.*' The theme of the 'heathen blackamore' was very popular. Professor Koeppel (in *Englische Studien,* 16. 370) points out several other versions of it: a Latin version by Pontano, an adaptation by Bandello in the twenty-first novel of his third book, a French paraphrase by Belleforest in the second volume of his *Histoires Tragiques.* And there are other versions in other languages.

When *Titus Andronicus* was entered on the Stationers' Register on February 6, 1593-4, there was entered also 'by warrant from Mr. Woodcock, the ballad thereof.' It is now generally agreed that this ballad is the same as that reprinted in Percy's *Reliques,* entitled *Titus Andronicus's Complaint,*[1] and that it is not a source of the play but instead is based on the play. It cannot, according to Chappell, be earlier, in its extant form, than 1600.

In connection with the question of the sources of the play, several other facts now enter. Henslowe in his Diary records a play, 'tittus & vespacia' (which he calls elsewhere 'tittus') as having been performed by

[1] See Appendix F, page 143.

Strange's men on April 11, 1592, and frequently thereafter. No copy of this play now exists. There is, furthermore, a volume, *Englische Comedien und Tragedien*, 1620, which comprises the repertory of a group of English comedians acting in Germany in the early seventeenth century, and which contains a play entitled *Eine sehr Klägliche Tragœdia von Tito Andronico und der hoffertigen Kayserin*.[1] In this play Titus's son is called Vespasianus instead of Lucius. It has been assumed, therefore, in some quarters that Henslowe's 'tittus & vespacia' was the original of the German play and at the same time an earlier version of our English *Titus Andronicus*.[2] But such assumptions are more or less gratuitous. There may have been an earlier play than our *Titus Andronicus* on the same subject. But in all probability the 'tittus & vespacia' of Henslowe had nothing to do with the play recorded elsewhere by him as 'titus & ondronicus' (our *Titus Andronicus*), but dealt instead with the heroic theme of the destruction of Jerusalem by Titus Vespasian, the second of the Flavian emperors, and the hero of later tragedies by Corneille and Racine. The German play is quite certainly a translation, albeit a very free one, of our *Titus Andronicus*. The fact that Titus's son, Lucius, is given the name Vespasian in the German play can be easily explained, as Mr. R. Crompton Rhodes points out (*Times Literary Supplement*, May 22, 1924): Lucius is the son of Titus and an emperor of

[1] Reprinted in Cohn's *Shakespeare in Germany*, 1865, pp. 156-235.

[2] There are extant also a Dutch play, *Aran en Titus*, by Jan Vos, printed first in 1642, and a program of a German play acted at Linz in 1699 which agrees substantially with the Dutch play. The connections and relations between these two plays, and the whole question of the relationship of the Shakespearean *Titus Andronicus* to continental plays on similar themes, is discussed at length by H. de W. Fuller and G. P. Baker in *Pub. Mod. Lang. Assn.*, 16. 1-76, 1901.

Rome, and the mental association of his name with Vespasian is explicable. The other changes of name in the German play have similarly associative reasons. Aaron the Moor becomes Morion, and Lavinia becomes Andronica.

About a quarter of a century ago there were numerous lengthy and learned discussions as to the existence of earlier versions and editions of *Titus Andronicus,* and the interrelations of the English, German, and Dutch versions of plays on similar themes. They were occasioned largely by the fact that until 1904 no copy of *Titus Andronicus* earlier than the Quarto of 1600 was known, and editors and commentators were much exercised to explain the identity of the 'titus & ondronicus' mentioned in Henslowe's Diary under date of January 23, 1594. Fortunately in 1904 a copy of the 1594 Quarto, the first edition of the play, came to light, settling many vexatious questions. It is now generally conceded that this 1594 edition of *Titus Andronicus* is the play recorded in Henslowe's Diary as 'titus & ondronicus' and that it is also identical with the 'Titus and Andronicus' and 'Tytus Andronicus' of the Stationers' Register.

APPENDIX B

The History of the Play

The earliest known mention of a work with the title of *Titus Andronicus* is contained in an entry in the Stationers' Register on February 6, 1593-4: 'John Danter. A booke entitled A noble Roman historye of Tytus Andronicus.' Philip Henslowe's Diary, under the dates of January 23 and 28, and February 6 of the same year, records a new play, 'titus & ondronicus,' as having been acted by 'the earle of susex his men.' Two later entries, made on June 5 and June 12, 1594, note the performance of a play called 'andronicous' by the Lord Admiral's and the Lord Chamberlain's men. Finally, in this same year, there was printed at London a quarto edition[1] of the play now known as *Titus Andronicus,* bearing the following title-page: 'The Most Lamentable Romaine Tragedie of Titus Andronicus: As it was Plaide by the Right Honourable the Earle of Darbie, Earle of Pembrooke, and Earle of Sussex their Servants. . . . London, Printed by Iohn Danter . . . 1594.'

A second quarto, based on the 1594 edition, was published in 1600, and contains only slight changes in the text. One passage of six lines is omitted from the first scene of the 1600 edition, and another of five lines is omitted from the last scene of the play (cf. notes on I. i. 35 and V. iii. 165), while the last four

---

[1] The 1594 Quarto of *Titus* was recorded by Gerard Langbaine in 1691 in the list of Shakespeare's plays in his *Account of the English Dramatick Poets,* but no copy of the edition seems to have been known during the next two hundred years, and Langbaine's testimony was generally discredited. At last, in 1904, a copy was discovered in Lund, Sweden, vindicating Langbaine, and settling various disputes.

lines of the 1600 edition are not found in the First
Quarto. On the title-page of the Second Quarto the
name of the Lord Chamberlain's company is added
to those of the three companies mentioned on the title-
page of the First Quarto.

A third quarto, of which the 1600 edition was the
original, was printed in 1611. Fourteen copies of the
Third Quarto are known, one of which is in the Elizabethan Club at Yale.

The text of the First Folio of 1623 was printed
from the Third Quarto with MS. additions, and contains one scene (III. ii.) which does not appear in
any of the Quartos.

The history of Titus and Aaron on the stage falls
into two general divisions: the period of about a
quarter of a century after its composition until the
death of Shakespeare, and the three centuries since
that time. During the first three decades of its existence, *Titus* was one of the most popular of all the
plays attributed to Shakespeare; for the last three
hundred years it has had almost the scantiest stage-
history of them all. The First Quarto bears the
motto, *Aut nunc aut nunquam,* and never was a more
appropriate motto affixed to a play. There was only
one period in the history of the English stage when
Titus Andronicus ever could have been popular, and
popular it was then beyond all precedent.

The title-page of the Third Quarto assures us that
the tragedy had 'sundry times beene plaide by the
Kings Majesties Servants,' and from the other title-
pages and Henslowe's Diary we learn that three different companies continued to play it, two of which
changed their names at two different periods of their
career; but under whatever name or sovereign, they
continued to play *Titus*. The play is entered in
Henslowe's Diary no less than fifteen times, if we
may assume that all the Titus and Andronicus plays

which he records are identical. Numerous other contemporary allusions also attest its popularity. The
events with which the first act of *Titus* concerns itself were familiar enough to furnish a simile for the
author of the play, *A Merry Knack to Know a
Knave*, which was published anonymously in 1594:

'*Osrick*. My gracious lord, as welcome shall you be,
 To me, my daughter, and my son-in-law,
 As Titus was unto the Roman senators,
 When he had made a conquest on the Goths;
 That, in requital of his service done,
 Did offer him the imperial diadem.
 As they in Titus, we in your grace, still find
 The perfect figure of a princely mind.'[1]

In 1614, twenty years after the First Quarto, Ben
Jonson takes occasion in the Induction to his *Bar-
tholomew Fair* to censure those (of whom there were
presumably a goodly number) who still 'swear that
Jeronimo or Andronicus are the best plays yet.'
Whether Jonson is referring to our *Titus Andronicus*
or not, the vogue of *Titus* would thus seem to have
passed by this time with men of Jonson's tastes, but
the contemptuous tone of his statement testifies that
there were those to whom such blood-and-thunder
plays still appealed. The *Shakspere Allusion-Book*
records other references to the play from time to
time. At the middle of the century strands of its gory
locks were still in evidence. In 1648 an anonymous
writer, J. S., issued a compilation of 'wise and learned
sentences and phrases' from favorite authors under
the title, *Wit's Labyrinth*. Of the half-dozen or more
Shakespearean plays from which the compiler culled
his phrases, only *Titus Andronicus* is honored by having as many as three sentences quoted.

As the century wore on, however, the performances

[1] Dodsley's *Old English Plays*, ed. Hazlitt, 1874, 6. 572.

of Titus grew fewer and fewer. In 1678, 'about the time of the Popish-plot,' says Gerard Langbaine, the play was 'revived' and refurbished to suit the tastes and exigencies of the stage, and produced by Edward Ravenscroft. This revised version of the tragedy was published in 1687 with the following title: *Titus Andronicus or the Rape of Lavinia. Acted at the Theatre Royall, A Tragedy Alter'd from Mr. Shakespear's Works.* In his introduction, Ravenscroft speaks of the success which had *matched* the labor of revising the play, a process which left *Titus* with 'the language not only refin'd, but many scenes entirely new: besides most of the principal characters heighten'd and the plot much encreas'd.' It is instructive to see in what manner the characters were 'heightened.' As if the original play were not horrible enough, Ravenscroft adds infanticide to Tamora's crimes, and has Aaron offer to eat his dead child's body. The Moor is tortured and finally burned to death on the stage.

Ravenscroft's revision was still the accepted version at the close of the century, according to the list of Shakespeare's plays given by Charles Gildon in 1698 in his continuation of Langbaine's work, previously mentioned. After the turn of the century we first hear definitely of a performance of *Titus* in 1717. There were at least three performances, on August 13, 20, and 23, of that year, at Drury Lane. The advertisement in the *Daily Courant* of the 20th states that the play had been given 'but twice these fifteen years.' The most interesting fact recorded in the notice is that the part of Aaron was taken by the celebrated James Quin, who repeated the performance again in 1720 and 1721, at Lincoln's Inn Fields. The version of Ravenscroft still obtained, the play being announced in all cases as 'Titus Andronicus with the Rape of Lavinia, alter'd from Shakspeare.'

A century and a quarter elapsed before Titus and
Aaron again walked the boards. Another much-
altered version of the text was used, prepared for the
occasion by C. A. Somerset, the author of *Shakespeare's Early Days,* a popular work of the time. The
play was performed at the Britannia Theatre in London, the opening performance taking place on March
15, 1852. In this new version, the tragedy was given
intermittently for some five years, with performances
both in London and Dublin. The rôle of Aaron was
taken by the famous negro tragedian, Ira Aldridge,
'the African Roscius.' Into the version employed by
Aldridge there was incorporated a scene from a play
called *Zaraffa, the Slave King,* which had been written especially for Aldridge.

It is significant with regard to the tastes of the au-
diences of the times that both in 1717 and in 1852 the
producers of *Titus* felt it necessary to follow the performance of the tragedy with a farce. In 1717, 'by
the desire of some Persons of Quality,' so the stage-
bill informs us, Farquhar's one-act farce, *The Stage-
Coach,* was added. In 1852 Aldridge offered a farce
entitled 'Mummy' and some negro songs which he had
brought from his native Maryland.

After 1857 it was sixty-six years before any pro-
ducer had the desire or the hardihood to present the
lamentable Roman tragedy. Under the management
of Miss Lilian Baylis, the entire cycle of Shakespeare's plays was given between 1914 and 1924 at
the Old Vic Theatre on the Surrey side of the Thames,
an achievement which had not been accomplished since
the days of Shakespeare. *Titus Andronicus* was produced here by Mr. Robert Atkins on October 8, 1923,
the thirty-fifth of the cycle of Shakespeare's thirty-
seven plays. That *Titus* should have been included
in the repertory is due, of course, not to any inherent
virtues in the play itself, but to Miss Baylis's ambi-

tion to make the Shakespearean wheel, for once at least, come full circle. A large audience was drawn to the Old Vic through curiosity, and the comments of the spectators and the newspapers were at one in declaring the play impossibly bad. The *Times* mentioned among the qualities which make it tolerable at all the swiftness and firmness of the telling, and the extraordinary dexterity with which the plot moves from death to death. 'It could never have appealed to the cultured classes,' said the *Morning Post,* 'but had all the elements of popular success. . . . It is very repulsive, but workmanlike.' The text used was the original version of the First Folio, with one noteworthy and very effective emendation: a laughing-scene for Aaron was introduced in Act III just before his exit, after he has cut off Titus's hand. The Moor's satanic laughter is not specifically referred to in the text, but is justified by his remarks. (Cf. V. i. 111–113.) A very fine stage-setting by Hubert Hine was used in the production at the Old Vic.

Titus has been produced only once in America. It was performed by the Yale Chapter of the Fraternity of Alpha Delta Phi, in New Haven, on April 14 and 15, 1924, under the direction of Mr. E. M. Woolley and Professor J. M. Berdan. The production was the annual performance of a series of Elizabethan plays, given in the Elizabethan manner, with the original text.

The Prinzregententheater in Munich was the scene of the latest performance of *Titus,* on October 15, 1924. The German version used was the translation of Nicolaus Delius, and very elaborate scenery by Eugen Keller was employed.

Titus Andronicus is the only play of the Shakespearean canon that has not been performed at the Shakespeare Memorial Theatre in Stratford.

APPENDIX C

The Authorship of the Play

The external evidence for the Shakespearean authorship of *Titus Andronicus* rests on its inclusion in the Folio of 1623 by Heminges and Condell, friends and fellow actors of Shakespeare, and its mention by Francis Meres in a list of Shakespeare's plays in his *Palladis Tamia* in 1598, four years after the appearance of the First Quarto. It is again listed as Shakespeare's by Gerard Langbaine[1] in 1691. Such evidence is not easily contestable, especially in view of the close connection between Shakespeare and the editors of the Folio, and the fact that Meres seems to have been sufficiently familiar with Shakespeare to have known of his privately circulated sonnets some eleven years before they were first printed. But in spite of these facts, the play, largely because of its repulsive theme, the crudeness of workmanship displayed throughout, the un-Shakespearean quality of many of its lines, and the presence in the text of numerous traces of the work of other authors, has been a storm-centre in Shakespearean criticism for over two centuries, and to-day it finds itself rejected, either partially or wholly, by far the greater number of editors and critics.

The first doubt as to Shakespeare's authorship of which we have any record is contained in the preface to Edward Ravenscroft's revision of the play in 1687, wherein he says: 'I have been told by some anciently conversant with the stage that it was not originally his, but brought by a private author to be acted, and he only gave some master-touches to one or two of the principal parts or characters; this I am apt to

[1] In the work referred to in Appendix B.

believe, because 't is the most incorrect and indigested piece in all his works. It seems rather a heap of rubbish than a structure.'

The integrity of Ravenscroft is discredited by Langbaine, who intimates that Ravenscroft was merely trying to belittle Shakespeare in order to exalt himself. He quotes part of the prologue which Ravenscroft originally prefixed to his revision of *Titus* in 1678, in which he called the play Shakespeare's and produced it as such, saying of his own part in it that he had

> 'but winnow'd Shakespeare's corn,
> So far he was from robbing him of 's treasure,
> That he did add his own, to make full measure.'

Ravenscroft's statement is, however, accepted in substance by the majority of critics since his day.

External evidence against Shakespeare's authorship of *Titus* has been found in the absence of his name from all three Quartos of the play. The conclusiveness of this evidence is impaired, however, by the fact that the poet's name does not appear on any of the Quartos of *Henry V*, or on any of the first three Quartos of *Romeo and Juliet*.

Eighteenth-century critics and editors, with the exception of Capell, denied the Shakespearean authorship of the play. Theobald thought Shakespeare might have added 'a few fine touches' to the play. Johnson, Farmer, and Steevens, reject the Shakespearean theory entirely. Johnson says of it: 'All the editors and critics agree in supposing this play spurious. I see no reason for differing from them; for the colour of the style is wholly different from that of the other plays, and there is an attempt at regular versification, and artificial closes, not always inelegant, yet seldom pleasing. The barbarity of the spectacles and the general massacre, which are here exhibited, can scarcely be conceived tolerable to any audience, yet we are told by Jonson that they were not only borne but praised. That Shakespeare wrote any part of it, though Theobald declares it *incontestable,* I see no reason for believing. . . . I do not find Shakespeare's touches very discernible.' Malone thought that Shakespeare might have written a few lines in the play, or perhaps have given some assistance to the author in revising it.

In the nineteenth century, critics were more widely divided in their opinions. Seymour, Drake, Singer, the Coleridges, Hallam, Dyce, Fleay, and others denied that Shakespeare had any part in its composition. Furnivall (Introduction to *Leopold Shakspere*), Ingleby (*Shakespeare: The Man and the Book*), Dowden (*Shakspere: His Mind and Art*), Herford (Introduction to *Eversley Shakespeare*), Hudson, and Rolfe, agreed that very little of the play could have been written by Shakespeare. On the other hand, a group of critics of whom we may name Collier (*Annals of the Stage,* 1831), Verplanck (*Illustrated Shakespeare,* 1847), Knight (*Pictorial Shakespeare,* 1867), Appleton Morgan (*Bankside Shakespeare,* 1890), and Crawford ('The Date and Authenticity of "Titus Andronicus," ' *Shakespeare Jahrbuch,* 1900), considered the play the work of Shakespeare, his earliest and crudest composition, produced when he was still under the influence of his predecessors. The latter view was concurred in almost unanimously by the German school: Schlegel, Delius, Bodenstedt, Franz Horn, Ulrici, Kurz, Sarrazin, Brandl, Creizenach, and Schröer. Gervinus, as in other matters of Shakespearean criticism, dissented from the opinion of his countrymen, and sided with the British school which denied Shakespeare's authorship of *Titus.*

The twentieth century brought with it the discovery of the First Quarto of *Titus,* and consequent fresh and lengthy discussions as to its authorship. There was a revival in certain quarters of the tendency to consider the play a work of Shakespeare's earlier days, and among the adherents of this opinion were Collins, Boas, Saintsbury, McCallum, and Raleigh. Courthope, in the appendix, 'On the Authenticity of Some of the Early Plays Assigned to Shakespeare, and their Relationship to the Development of his Dramatic Genius,' to his *History of English Poetry,* vol. iv, 1903, espouses the theory of the Shakespearean authorship of *Titus.* His formal conclusion is 'That there are no sufficient internal reasons to warrant us in resisting the testimony of the folio of 1623 that *Titus Andronicus* and *King Henry VI.* are the work of Shakespeare.' Greg, in his edition of Henslowe's Diary (II. 161), gives his opinion of the circumstances of Shakespeare's connection with *Titus:* 'I fail to discover any clear internal evidence of Shakespeare having touched the play at all, though there are a few lines whose Shakespearian authorship I do not think impossible. . . . The Chamberlain's men, following their practice in the case of the other Pembroke's plays, *Hamlet* and the *Taming of a Shrew,* caused *Titus* to be worked over by a young member of their company named William Shakespeare. Thus revised the piece achieved sufficient success to call for notice by Francis Meres in 1598, and thenceforth passed as one of the "works" of the favourite playwright-actor. This MS. perished in the fire at the Globe in 1613. Wishing to replace their prompt copy the King's men procured a copy of the printed edition (1611), a device to which they certainly resorted in other cases too. In this they made certain alterations in the stage directions, and in doing so noticed the absence of one scene at least (III. ii.) which they were in the habit of acting and which had proved popular. This the actors were able to reconstruct from memory, and a manuscript insertion of some 85 lines was made in the quarto. Ten years later this doctored prompt copy was sent to press for the text of the collected folio.'

So far as there may be said to be a prevailing theory among American students, it is that Shakespeare is the reviser, to some extent, of an older play. But as to the author or authors of the original work, and as to the nature and extent of the revision, there is considerable latitude of opinion. Among American students of the play there are to be mentioned Schelling, Fuller, Baker, Wendell, Stoll, H. D. Gray, and Parrott. J. Q. Adams, in his *Life of Shakespeare,* 1923 (p. 134), pictures Shakespeare shortly after the death of Marlowe 'exercising his skill in touching up several of the old stock pieces belonging to the company, plays, no doubt, in which he himself had been called upon to act. Perhaps one of these was *Titus Andronicus,* mainly, if not entirely, by George Peele. . . . Shakespeare could hardly have had a genuine artistic interest in the bloody *Titus,* but his business shrewdness showed him the opportunity of turning it into a great money-maker for his company.'

The two lengthiest recent discussions of the authorship of the play are by H. B. Baildon (*Arden Shakespeare,* 1904), who believes the play to be substantially and essentially the work of Shakespeare, and J. M. Robertson, whose elaborate study, *Did Shakespeare Write 'Titus Andronicus'?,* 1905, revised in 1924 as *An Introduction to the Study of the Shakespeare Canon, Proceeding on the Problem of 'Titus Andronicus,'* rejects *in toto* the theory that the play is the work of Shakespeare.

The arguments concerning the Shakespearean authorship of *Titus* turn largely on the consideration of questions of the metrical construction, versification, vocabulary, characters, theme, and general style of the play. Few hard and fast conclusions can be drawn from all the evidence produced, however, as there is little agreement among critics as to its proper interpretation. Studies of the metre of the play, with special attention to the number of double and triple endings, riming lines, and the quality of the blank verse employed in it, have been made in endeavors to throw light on the question of authorship, but nothing definitely conclusive has come of it, so varied are the constructions placed upon the data obtained. Again, the elaborate investigations of the style of the play and the innumerable similarities of idea and expression between *Titus* and other Elizabethan plays have resulted in the discovery of much valuable information as to the wholesale borrowings of the writers of the time, but the findings are construed in widely different ways. What seems to one critic or school convincing evidence of Shakespearean workmanship, is often quite as convincing to another that Shakespeare had nothing to do with the play. Flügel, for instance, thought Aaron as un-Shakespearean as could be, whereas Saintsbury, Collins, Parrott, and others have found him genuinely Shakespearean. Schröer and Parrott, again, consider the classical allusions quite in Shakespeare's manner; but, says Robertson, who finds the classical allusions thoroughly pre-Shakespearean, 'what is obviously non-Shakespearean is the classicism of the play.' Not only are the critics in disagreement with one another, but they are not consistent with themselves. Schröer, whose study, *Über Titus Andronicus,* 1891, is the most comprehensive of the German arguments advocating Shakespeare's authorship of the play, contends, as Robertson notes, that 'verbal coincidence between two poems speaks rather against than for identity of authorship—' (p. 73), and yet some fifty-two pages later he argues that Aaron's praise of blackness (IV. ii. 72,

100) is a favorite idea with Shakespeare, because we have it again in *Love's Labour's Lost* (V. ii. 20, 41).

The attempts at choosing what in the play is genuinely Shakespearean, as distinguished from what may be considered the work of his supposed collaborators, have not met with any greater success. Almost every editor who accepts in part the Shakespearean hypothesis has his favorite list of selections which he believes authentic. Such passages consist in most cases of the more lyrical sections, and include, of course, all the better lines of the tragedy. But there is a remarkable disagreement among them, and such selections, if put together properly, would constitute almost the whole of the play. Coleridge, from a poet's point of view, considered as worthy of Shakespeare only some forty lines from the 'Revenge' scene (V. ii. 20-60), whereas Swinburne, from another poet's point of view, disregarded all but the 'Clown' scene (IV. iii.). The one scene on which there has been more general agreement, perhaps, than on any other, is the second scene of Act III, which appeared for the first time in the Folio, and therefore attracts attention to itself as having perhaps come from Shakespeare's own copy or his MSS. The whole process of picking and choosing must be considered futile, however, and especially since half of the passages tagged as certainly Shakespearean have been shown to be similar to, or identical with, passages in Peele, Greene, Marlowe, and others.

Nor do we find any grounds for more definite conclusions when we examine the passages in *Titus* which are most strikingly suggestive of lines and scenes in Shakespeare's authenticated works. The theme of *Lucrece* is similar to that of the plot in which Lavinia figures, but we cannot therefore conclude that Shakespeare is necessarily the author of *Titus* because he is the author of *Lucrece*. The poem may, in-

deed, have been suggested by the play, or the play by
the poem, but identity of authorship is no more requi-
site in such a supposition than it is if we suppose the
plot of Shylock to have been suggested by Marlowe's
Jew of Malta. It must be admitted that Aaron's lines
(IV. ii. 102, 103),

> 'For all the water in the ocean
> Can never turn the swan's black legs to white,'

suggest those of *Richard II* (III. ii. 54, 55),

> 'Not all the water in the rough rude sea
> Can wash the balm off from an anointed king,'

and still further the cry of Lady Macbeth (*Macbeth*,
II. ii. 60, 61),

> 'Will all great Neptune's ocean wash this blood
> Clean from my hand?'

But we are not justified in concluding that the author
of the two later passages is necessarily the author of
the first. Shakespeare was as imitative as he was re-
petitive, even if we assume that he had Aaron's lines
in mind when he was composing the two later passages.

There is a clear verbal parallel between lines in
Tamora's speech (II. iii. 17-19),

> 'And, whilst the babbling echo mocks the hounds,
> Replying shrilly to the well-tun'd horns,
> As if a double hunt were heard at once, . . .'

and two lines (695-696) of *Venus and Adonis,*

> 'Thus do they [the hounds] spend their mouths: Echo replies
> As if another chase were in the skies.'

As Parrott points out,[1] these parallels, and others

---

[1] 'Shakespeare's Revision of "Titus Andronicus," ' *Mod.
Lang. Rev.,* xiv. 27, 28.

which he gives, are unmistakable, and he accordingly assigns the paralleled lines and Tamora's speech to Shakespeare; but, as Robertson observes, it does not follow necessarily that Shakespeare must himself have written Tamora's speech. Any of his contemporaries would have copied such a fine passage without scruple if he had wished to do so.

The studies of the characters of the play in relation to those of others of Shakespeare's plays have been no more conclusive in their results. Aaron, for example, is quite generally considered, by all who uphold Shakespeare's intimate connection with the play, as a first draft and prototype of Shylock, Iago, Richard III, Edmund, and most of Shakespeare's villains. It is by external and superficial implications, however, rather than by inherent likenesses that he is connected with them. He is a Moor, and the tragedy of *Othello the Moor* is at once suggested, wherein, as it happens, there is Iago, a villain in the popular sense, and certain similarities in the characters of Iago and Aaron begin to appear. But fundamentally and essentially Aaron and Iago are not of the same stripe. Aaron is pre-Shakespearean rather than Shakespearean, and belongs to the tribe of Tamburlaine, Barabas, Ithamore, Eleazar, and Peele's Moor, Muly Muhamet, rather than to that of Iago. His melodramatic rant and braggadocio, and his comic-opera frenzy for evil-doing, form a striking contrast to the tragically sinister and motiveless malignity of Iago. As for his relation to Shylock, is not the apparent connection between them based subconsciously on the circumstance of their being members respectively of races alike alien and despised from the Elizabethan point of view? Similarities and parallels between Tamora, and the Margaret of the *Henry VI* trilogy (who is fundamentally non-Shakespearean), on the one hand, and Lady Macbeth on the other, seem equally superficial. The

three have little in common but their imperiousness.
The treatment of the character of Titus certainly does
not suggest Shakespeare's handling of the characters
of Lear, Othello, and Macbeth. Nor does young
Lucius seem to have more than his tender years in
common with Prince Arthur and the young princes of
Richard III. There is, however, one character, the
Clown, in *Titus,* who is quite in the manner and tradi-
tion of Shakespeare, but even he is not distinctively
and exclusively Shakespearean. Elizabethan and
Tudor drama have clowns and to spare, and the clown
of *Titus* is not more like the clowns of Shakespeare
than he is like those of his contemporaries. But he is
the one typically Shakespearean thing in the entire
play, and he may very well be conceded to Shakespeare as being of a piece with Launce, Launcelot
Gobbo, and Elbow, and as constituting one of the
'master-touches' which Ravenscroft represents Shakespeare as imparting to the play.

Previous study of characters, metre, phrasing, and
general stylistic qualities cannot, therefore, be said to
have produced any conclusive or convincing reasons
for considering *Titus* Shakespeare's. The work of
critics, ranging from the early observations of
Steevens and Malone down to the exhaustive researches of Robertson, have proved that the play is a
collection of materials drawn from a common stock
used by all Elizabethan dramatists, and that, in particular, it is a tissue of words, phrases, and sentiments
taken largely from Peele, Greene, Kyd, Marlowe, and
Lodge. The author, or authors, of *Titus Andronicus,*
whoever they were, simply followed the common habit
of turning to other authors and similar works: what
they thought they might require, they went and took to
furnish out a lamentable Roman tragedy.

Close examination of the text of *Titus,* therefore,
reveals no more reason for including it in the canon of

Shakespeare's plays than could be found for including many of those pre-Shakespearean plays with which it is organically and spiritually connected—the *Spanish Tragedy, Lust's Dominion, Selimus,* the *Battle of Alcazar,* the *Troublesome Reign,* the *Chronicle History of King Leir,* and others.

But it is not merely or chiefly the negative argument—that *Titus* is lacking in distinctive and convincing Shakespearean characteristics—that justifies the rejection of the play as Shakespeare's, but the more fundamental and positive fact that it contains much that is certainly not Shakespeare's and that is as certainly the work of other Elizabethans. That the version of the play which was printed in the 1594 Quarto could not have been completed earlier than the middle of the year 1593 is proved by the fact that it copies directly or indirectly many phrases and passages of Peele's *Honour of the Garter,* which was written to celebrate an event that occurred on June 26, 1593; and yet the language, the metre, and the style of *Titus* is noticeably different from that of the works which Shakespeare had already written and was writing during this particular period—the *Comedy of Errors, Love's Labour's Lost, Two Gentlemen of Verona, Richard III,* and *A Midsummer Night's Dream,* and the poems, *Venus and Adonis* and *Lucrece.* As late as 1593 he would hardly have written such bad lines or constructed so poor a play. If he had written it as early as 1589 or 1590, he could hardly have written in a style so wholly unlike that of the *Comedy of Errors* and *Love's Labour's Lost,* which he was presumably engaged in composing at that time.

Moreover, the language of *Titus* is shot through with words and expressions which Shakespeare did not use in any of his unquestioned works. A list of these words peculiar to *Titus,* first begun by Fleay,

and corrected and added to by Grosart, Verity, and
latterly by Robertson, contains upwards of a hundred terms which are the common property of Peele,
Greene, and Kyd, respectively, but are never used by
Shakespeare. If to these be added the host of classical allusions and tags found in *Titus* and in no other
Shakespearean work, the linguistic medium of the play
becomes a thing apart in the language of the Shakespearean canon.

But more fundamental than all these considera-
tions of style, metre, vocabulary, and characterization,
is the fact that the theme and the author's handling of
it, and the general atmosphere and spirit of *Titus Andronicus,* are wholly unlike and utterly alien to anything we have of Shakespeare, or could expect from
him. A theme of such unmitigated horror never appealed to Shakespeare in his later career as a dramatist, and least of all could it have appealed to the
young Shakespeare of *Love's Labour's Lost* and the
Midsummer Night's Dream. He came closest to such
themes in *Romeo and Juliet* in the year following the
first publication of *Titus,* and in *Hamlet,* a few years
later, and his method of handling them in those plays is
the best evidence of what he could do and would do with
the type of tragedy bequeathed to him by Seneca and
Kyd. In none of his tragedies does he deal with blood
for blood's sake, but in *Titus* there is no relief from
blood-letting, either by the inevitable Shakespearean
interspersion of comic scenes, or by the interjection of
another and more romantic plot. Horrors are heaped
on horrors in a way that would have sickened the senti-
mental author of Shakespeare's early plays, and would
have disgusted the author of *Othello* and *King Lear.*
And all to no purpose. In *Romeo and Juliet,* the
tragedy and the bloodshed result in the burying of
the parents' strife; in *Othello,* it is the cause which
leads a man great of heart to slay Desdemona, not

without recognizing the pity of it; in *King Lear,* the
evil consumes itself, and a clear morning follows the
storm of passion and tragedy. But in *Titus Andronicus* it is all

> 'Irrecoverably dark, total eclipse
> Without all hope of day.'

The tragic energy all goes for nothing; Titus's madness is without any redeeming element. Shakespeare
might have been capable of producing the bad lines
of the play, its crude construction, its feeble characterization, and its poor workmanship in general, but
that he could have written at any time a play so wholly
unlike any of his other work seems incredible. If
Titus Andronicus be Shakespeare's, we shall have to
posit a complete change in his mental, spiritual, and
artistic processes and attitudes between the time of its
composition and the date when he began to produce
his other dramatic work.

If Shakespeare, then, did not write *Titus,* who was
the author of the piece? Any one of a half-dozen of
his contemporaries is a more likely candidate for the
questionable honor. Its Senecanism and melodrama
it has in common with a score of other tragedies of
the time. Its mannerisms of style, versification, and
vocabulary are those of Kyd, Marlowe, Greene, Peele,
and Lodge. Accordingly, four at least of these have
been suggested as its possible author, and none of
them has wanted defenders among the critics to make
good his claim.

In the process of looking for specific traces of different hands in the play, however, many difficulties
present themselves. Some idea of the general state
of criticism with regard to this particular matter may
be gained from a glance at the various interpretations
placed on a single passage from Aaron's speech (II.
i. 1-9):

> 'Now climbeth Tamora Olympus' top,
> Safe out of Fortune's shot; and sits aloft,
> Secure of thunder's crack or lightning flash,
> Advanc'd above pale envy's threat'ning reach.
> As when the golden sun salutes the morn,
> And, having gilt the ocean with his beams,
> Gallops the zodiac in his glistering coach,
> And overlooks the highest-peering hills;
> So Tamora.'

Bullen, in his edition of Marlowe's plays, was of the opinion that this passage was written by Marlowe, in view of Marlowe's having written, in the third chorus of Act III of *Faustus,* the line,

> 'Did mount himself to scale Olympus' top.'

Appleton Morgan (*Bankside Shakespeare*) thinks the passage Shakespeare's without question, and considers it a remarkably good imitation of Marlowe's style. Crawford, however, sees in lines 3-5 of the passage an echo of Peele's *Honour of the Garter* (line 410),

> 'Out of Oblivion's reach or Envy's shot,'

while Robertson finds in line 7 a direct echo of a line from Peele's *Anglorum Feriæ,*

> 'Gallops the zodiac in his fiery wain,'

and notes other lines from Peele's *David and Bethsabe* strikingly parallel in structure and abounding in verbal coincidences. Such resemblances are, indeed, very striking, but do they definitely prove more than that there was a singular community of thought and similarity of expression, and no little amount of imitation, among Elizabethan poets? And what, to give only one instance, shall be said of the lines in the *Merchant of Venice* (IV. i. 9, 10),

> 'no lawful means can carry me
> Out of his envy's reach'?

That they are Shakespeare's has never been questioned, but if they had occurred in *Titus,* would they not certainly be catalogued as Peele's or Marlowe's by just such reasoning? If mere similarity or identity of thought or expression is to be accepted as a criterion of authorship, then almost any Elizabethan dramatist may be proved to have written parts of almost any play of the time.

The play is so patently of the same species as the *Spanish Tragedy,* that Kyd was early suggested by Farmer as author of *Titus.* Hartley Coleridge concurred in this, and Fleay, Sir Sidney Lee, Parrott, and Robertson have since thought Kyd a probable first draftsman of the play. Boswell preferred to consider Marlowe, and Fleay also inclined to this opinion. The character of Aaron is by almost all critics conceded to be modeled on Marlowe's Barabas and Ithamore. Much of the verse also, if not Marlowe's, is close imitation of that poet's lines. The share of Robert Greene in *Titus* has received more attention than that of any other of the possible authors except Peele. In a long and scholarly article[1] Grosart set forth his many claims to the authorship, and he has received the serious consideration of every critic since. The play unquestionably contains much that was written by Greene, but whether his passages got into it by his own pen, or whether his imitators put them there is a problem that cannot be solved. Parrott and Robertson agree substantially in conceding to Greene's authorship the first scene of Act II, and traces of his manner are not wanting throughout the play. Grant White thought *Titus* was written by Greene, Marlowe, and Shakespeare, and later revised by Shakespeare.

But of all those for whom the authorship of *Titus*

[1] 'Was Robert Greene Substantially the Author of "Titus Andronicus"?' *Englische Studien,* xxii. 389-436.

is claimed, George Peele is the foremost. His influence and his mannerisms are evident throughout the play, which is as Peelean in spirit as it is non-Shakespearean. Indeed, if the play were not specially credited to Shakespeare, there can be little doubt that it would be readily assigned to Peele by the majority of students of Elizabethan drama. 'Almost every page,' says Dugdale Sykes, 'exhibits traces of Peele's vocabulary and phrasing.'[1] At least one third of the entire play has been shown to be directly or indirectly copied from his works. The most important developments in the study and criticism of *Titus* during the present century have centered in the question of Peele's connection with the play, and to the earlier proofs of Fleay, Verity, and Crawford of his great share in its text, abundant evidence has been added by the exhaustive researches of Sykes and Robertson. J. Q. Adams adheres to the theory of Peele's authorship of the play in his *Life*, and it is not unreasonable to expect that future critics may consider the evidence sufficient to establish his claim to the play. When all allowances are made for the Elizabethan tendency toward imitation of other works, the play still remains characteristically Peelean, exhibiting all his sentimentality, his weakness for rodomontade, his fondness for the historical background in tragedy, his peculiar interest in Oriental themes, his love of martial exploits and exploiters, and his glorification of the fatherland, identical here with Rome, as it is in *David and Bethsabe* with Judæa. Surely there was no one so likely as Peele to have chosen such a subject for a tragedy, and, given the theme here found, there can be little doubt that he would have written substantially what we have in *Titus Andronicus*.

What conclusions, then, are to be drawn from all the mass of critical discussion on the authorship of

[1] *Sidelights on Shakespeare*, 1919, p. 125.

Titus Andronicus, and the scores of conflicting interpretations and opinions of the play which have arisen
during the two centuries and a half since Ravenscroft gave to the world the story of the 'private author'? There are certain general conclusions that do
no violence to such facts as we have, and can be
brought into reasonable conformity with the evidence
available. First, the tragedy as it stands in the Folio
of 1623 does not seem at all Shakespearean in substance, or treatment, or spirit. What we know of the
mind and the tastes of Shakespeare forbids the ascrip-
tion of this play to his pen, even as its earliest and
crudest production. Secondly, from what is known
of the manner, tastes, and workmanship of his contemporaries, the presumption is that George Peele
is substantially the author of *Titus Andronicus,* with
assistance, perhaps, from Robert Greene. Thirdly,
the fact that the play was listed as Shakespeare's by
Meres, and was printed as Shakespeare's in the Folio
by Heminges and Condell, warrants the conclusion
that Shakespeare retouched it to some extent. And
thus we arrive, by a most circuitous process of reasoning, exactly where the controversy started, with
Ravenscroft's statement in 1687. The most that
Shakespeare could have had to do with *Titus Andronicus* is, we must believe, no more than what those
'anciently conversant with the stage' gave as their
testimony—'he only gave some master-touches to one
or two of the principal parts or characters.'

APPENDIX D

The Text of the Present Edition

The text of the present volume is, by permission of the Oxford University Press, that of the Oxford Shakespeare, edited by the late W. J. Craig, except for the following deviations:

1. The stage directions of the First Folio have been restored, necessary modern additions being enclosed in square brackets. Passages of text for which the Folio offers no equivalent are similarly bracketed.

2. Many minor changes in punctuation have been made, and the spelling of certain words normalized in accordance with English usage; e.g. everything, swoll'n, villainy. The old forms, murther, murtherer, etc., which occur in the Folio beside murder, murderer, etc., have been retained.

3. The following alterations, most of them reversions to the readings of the First Folio, have been made in the text, the reading of the present text preceding the colon, and that of Craig following it:

I. i.	108	sons F: son
	126	T'appease F: to appease
	154	grudges F: drugs
	487	sware F: swore
II. i.	25	Hollo! F: Holla!
iii.	55	whom F: who
	126	braves F: she braves
iv.	17	Hath F: have
III. i.	12	these, tribunes F: these, these, tribunes
	36	And bootless,: All bootless
	225	flow F: blow
	259	my F: thy
ii.	9	Who, when F: And when
	60	'But!' How, if that fly had a father and mother?: But how if that fly had a father and a mother?
	85	begin F: begins

IV. i. 45	so busily she turns the leaves! Help her. F: see how busily she turns the leaves! [*Helping her.*
77	ye F: you
129	Revenge the heavens F: Revenge, ye heavens,
ii. 63	she is F: she's
150	Lord F: lord
164	ye F: you
iii. 2	let me see F: now let me see
8	Haply F: Happily
67	Ha, ha! F: Ha!
117	an humble suppliant F: a humble suppliant
118	given it the emperor F: given it to the emperor
iv. 2	emperor in Rome F: emperor of Rome
30	Th'effects F: The effects
61	Arm, my lords. F: Arm, arm, my lord.
71	begins F: begin
92	food F: feed
V. i. 61	And if F: An if
88	luxurious F: luxurious and
119	sounded F: swounded
ii. 30	th'infernal F: the infernal
40	offenders F: offender
49	globes F: globe
50	Provide thee F: Provide
62	Rape F: Rapine
137	bide F: abide
196	Progne F: Procne
203	might F: may
205	I'll F: I will
iii. 1	'tis F: it is
11	my F: mine
38	enforc'd F: enforced
48	hast F: hast thou
52	now is F: is now
68	uproars F: uproar
96	This F: then
109	I am turn'd forth F: I am the turn'd forth

APPENDIX E

The First Illustration to 'Shakespeare'

The drawing and script reproduced at the head of this edition of *Titus Andronicus* is of special interest as the first known illustration to any play of the Shakespearean canon. It is from the pen of Henry Peacham, artist, schoolmaster, epigrammatist, and pamphleteer, and was discovered by Sir E. K. Chambers in Volume I of the *Harley Papers* at Longleat.

The document, dating from 1595, is important as indicating that the Elizabethans regarded Moors as coal-black, not tawny. In the drawing, Tamora is represented kneeling before Titus, pleading for the life of her sons. Two bound figures, presumably her sons, kneel behind her, and Aaron the Moor stands beside them. The figures behind Titus are supposedly the executioners. The only known text to which Peacham could have had access is the First Quarto of 1594. The text of the MS. is an arrangement of lines from the speeches of Tamora and Titus (I. i. 104-121) and of Aaron (V. i. 125-144), with an interpolation of two lines and a half for Titus which are not found in any of the printed texts. Peacham has supplied his own stage directions. Certain minor variations between the lines of the MS. and those of the printed texts are noticeable, and the possibility of an earlier version of the play might thence be inferred. There seems to be some confusion as to whether the death of only one son (Alarbus) or of more than one is contemplated. Titus's lines, as well as Tamora's last line, seem to indicate that only one is to be put to death, and this circumstance agrees substantially with the texts of the versions which we have. Chambers thinks that the drawing clearly indicates that both sons are to be put to death, but this does not seem necessarily to be the purport of the illustration.

The text of the dialogue accompanying the drawing reads as follows:

Enter Tamora pleadinge for her sonnes going to execution

Tam: Stay Romane bretheren gratious Conquerors
Victorious Titus rue the teares I shed
A mothers teares in passion of her sonnes
And if thy sonnes were ever deare to thee
Oh thinke my sonnes to bee as deare to mee
Suffizeth not that wee are brought to Roome
To beautify thy triumphes and returne
Captiue to thee and to thy Romane yoake
But must my sonnes be slaughtered in the streetes
for valiant doinges in there Cuntryes cause
Oh if to fight for kinge and Common weale
Were piety in thine it is in these
Andronicus staine not thy tombe *with* blood
Wilt thou drawe neere the nature of the God*es*
Drawe neere them then in being mercifull
Sweete mercy is nobilityes true badge
Thrice noble Titus spare my first borne sonne

Titus: Patient your self madame for dy hee must
Aaron do you likewise prepare your selfe
And now at last repent your wicked\life

Aron: Ah now I curse the day and yet I thinke
few comes within the compasse of my curse
Wherein I did not some notorious ill
As kill a man or els devise his death
Ravish a mayd or plott the way to do it
Acuse some innocent and forsweare my selfe
Set deadly enmity betweene too freend*es*
Make poore mens cattell breake theire neckes
Set fire on barnes and haystackes in the night
And bid the owners quench them *with* their teares

Oft have I digd vp dead men from their graves
And set them vpright at their deere frend*es* dore
Even almost when theire sorrowes was forgott
And on their brestes as on the barke of trees
Have with my knife carvd in Romane letters
Lett not your sorrowe dy though I am dead
Tut I have done a thousand dreadfull thinges
As willingly as one would kill a fly
And nothing greives mee hartily indeede
for that I cannot doo ten thousand more & *cetera*
Alarbus[1]

[1] The manuscript breaks off here. It was apparently the intention of Peacham to give a speaking part to Alarbus, who is without a speech in the extant editions of *Titus*.

APPENDIX F

The following ballad, referred to in Appendix A, is found in Book II of the first volume of Percy's *Reliques*. 'Throughout the ballad,' says Grant White, 'there is evident effort to compress all the incidents of the story within as brief a relation as possible; and this is not the style of a ballad written for the ballad's sake.'

TITUS ANDRONICUS'S COMPLAINT

You noble minds, and famous martiall wights,
That in defence of native country fights,
Give eare to me, that ten yeeres fought for Rome,
Yet reapt disgrace at my returning home.

In Rome I lived in fame fulle threescore yeeres,
My name beloved was of all my peeres;
Full five and twenty valiant sonnes I had,
Whose forwarde vertues made their father glad.

For when Rome's foes their warlike forces bent,
Against them stille my sonnes and I were sent;
Against the Goths full ten yeeres weary warre
We spent, receiving many a bloudy scarre.

Just two and twenty of my sonnes were slaine
Before we did returne to Rome againe:
Of five and twenty sonnes, I brought but three
Alive, the stately towers of Rome to see.

When wars were done, I conquest home did bring,
And did present my prisoners to the king,
The queene of Goths, her sons, and eke a moore,
Which did such murders, like was nere before.

The emperour did make this queene his wife,
Which bred in Rome debate and deadlie strife;
The moore, with her two sonnes did growe soe proud,
That none like them in Rome might bee allowd.

The moore soe pleas'd this new-made empress' eie,
That she consented to him secretlye
For to abuse her husbands marriage bed,
And soe in time a blackamore she bred.

Then she, whose thoughts to murder were inclinde,
Consented with the moore of bloody minde
Against myselfe, my kin, and all my friendes,
In cruell sort to bring them to their endes.

Soe when in age I thought to live in peace,
Both care and griefe began then to increase:
Amongst my sonnes I had one daughter bright,
Which joy'd, and pleased best my aged sight:

My deare Lavinia was betrothed than
To Cesars sonne, a young and noble man:
Who in a hunting by the emperours wife
And her two sonnes, bereaved was of life.

He being slaine, was cast in cruel wise,
Into a darksome den from light of skies:
The cruell moore did come that way as then
With my three sonnes, who fell into the den.

The moore then fetcht the emperour with speed,
For to accuse them of that murderous deed;
And when my sonnes within the den were found,
In wrongfull prison they were cast and bound.

But nowe, behold! what wounded most my mind,
The empresses two sonnes of savage kind
My daughter ravished without remorse,
And took away her honour, quite perforce.

When they had tasted of soe sweete a flowre,
Fearing this sweete should shortly turn to sowre,
They cutt her tongue, whereby she could not tell
How that dishonoure unto her befell.

Then both her hands they basely cutt off quite,
Whereby their wickednesse she could not write;
Nor with her needle on her sampler sowe
The bloudye workers of her direfull woe.

My brother Marcus found her in the wood,
Staining the grassie ground with purple bloud,
That trickled from her stumpes, and bloudlesse armes:
Noe tongue at all she had to tell her harmes.

But when I sawe her in that woefull case,
With teares of bloud I wet mine aged face:
For my Lavinia I lamented more
Then for my two and twenty sonnes before.

When as I sawe she could not write nor speake,
With grief mine aged heart began to breake;
We spred an heape of sand upon the ground,
Whereby those bloudy tyrants out we found.

For with a staffe, without the helpe of hand,
She writt these wordes upon the plat of sand:
"The lustfull sonnes of the proud emperesse
Are doers of this hateful wickednesse."

I tore the milk-white hairs from off mine head,
I curst the houre wherein I first was bred,
I wisht this hand, that fought for countrie's fame,
In cradle rockt, had first been stroken lame.

The moore delighting still in villainy
Did say, to sett my sonnes from prison free
I should unto the king my right hand give,
And then my three imprisoned sonnes should live.

The moore I caused to strike it off with speede,
Whereat I grieved not to see it bleed,
But for my sonnes would willingly impart,
And for their ransome send my bleeding heart.

But as my life did linger thus in paine,
They sent to me my bootlesse hand againe,
And therewithal the heades of my three sonnes,
Which filld my dying heart with fresher moanes.

Then past reliefe I upp and downe did goe,
And with my teares writ in the dust my woe:
I shot my arrowes towards heaven hie,
And for revenge to hell often did crye.

The empresse then, thinking that I was mad,
Like Furies she and both her sonnes were clad,
(She nam'd Revenge, and Rape and Murder they)
To undermine and heare what I would say.

I fed their foolish veines a certaine space,
Untill my friendes did find a secret place,
Where both her sonnes unto a post were bound,
And just revenge in cruell sort was found.

I cut their throates, my daughter held the pan
Betwixt her stumpes, wherein the bloud it ran:
And then I ground their bones to powder small,
And made a paste for pyes streight therewithall.

Then withe their fleshe I made two mighty pyes,
And at a banquet served in stately wise:
Before the empresse set this lothsome meat;
So of her sonnes own flesh she well did eat.

Myself bereav'd my daughter then of life,
The empresse then I slewe with bloudy knife,
And stabb'd the emperour immediatelie,
And then myself: even soe did Titus die.

Then this revenge against the moore was found,
Alive they sett him halfe into the ground,
Whereas he stood untill such time he starv'd.
And soe God send all murderers may be serv'd.

APPENDIX G

SUGGESTIONS FOR COLLATERAL READING

A. C. Symons: Introduction to Prætorius Facsimile of 1600 Quarto of *Titus Andronicus*, 1886.

Henrietta C. Bartlett and Alfred W. Pollard: *A Census of Shakespeare's Plays in Quarto*, 1594-1709, 1916. (An invaluable source of information with regard to bibliographical details of the play.)

J. W. Cunliffe: *The Influence of Seneca on Elizabethan Tragedy*, 1893. (An informative discussion of the major influence in *Titus* and kindred tragedies.)

Tucker Brooke: *The Tudor Drama*, 1911, pp. 206-222. (An appraisal of *Titus* in its relation to similar plays of the period.)

F. S. Boas: *Shakspere and his Predecessors*, 1896. (An examination of the more immediate influences on the play.)

W. W. Greg: *Henslowe's Diary*, 1904-1908. (A valuable critical commentary on Henslowe's records of the play, with an illuminating discussion of its authorship, II. 159-162.)

F. G. Fleay: *Life and Work of Shakespeare*, 1886, pp. 280-282. (A rejection of the Shakespearean authorship of *Titus* based on the internal evidence of the play.)

Albert Cohn: *Shakespeare in Germany*, 1865. (A discussion, with English and German versions, of the *Titus Andronicus* performed by English players in Germany in 1620. I. cxii-cxiii, II. 156-235.)

H. de W. Fuller: 'The Sources of "Titus Andronicus."' In *Pub. Mod. Lang. Assn. of America*, 1901, pp. 1-65. (A very scholarly and ingenious comparison of the Dutch and German versions of the play with the English version, the conclusions being not altogether convincing.)

G. P. Baker: ' "Tittus and Vespacia" and "Titus and Ondronicus" in Henslowe's Diary.' In *Pub. Mod. Lang. Assn. of America,* 1901, pp. 66-76. (A sequel to the foregoing article.)

Arnold Schröer: *Über Titus Andronicus,* 1891. (The most comprehensive of the German treatises in favor of the Shakespearean authorship of *Titus.*)

A. B. Grosart: 'Was Robert Greene Substantially the Author of "Titus Andronicus"?' In *Englische Studien,* xxii. 389-436, 1896. (A very interesting and important document in the study of the authorship of the play.)

Charles Crawford: 'The Date and Authenticity of "Titus Andronicus." ' In *Jahrbuch der deutschen Shakespeare-Gesellschaft,* xxxvi. 109-121, 1900. (A thesis on Shakespeare's imitation of Peele in *Titus.*)

W. J. Courthope: *A History of English Poetry,* Vol. 4, 1903. (The Appendix, 'On the Authenticity of Some of the Early Plays Assigned to Shakespeare,' pp. 455-476, concludes that the internal evidence supports the external evidence in testifying that the play is Shakespeare's.)

J. Churton Collins: *Studies in Shakespeare,* 1904, pp. 96-120. (Asserts the authenticity of *Titus* on the ground of its similarity to others of Shakespeare's tragedies. The parallels seem forced in many instances.)

William Sharp: 'Titus Andronicus.' In *Harper's Magazine,* October, 1909, pp. 747-754. (Fiona MacLeod contends *a priori* that Shakespeare barely retouched the play, if at all. Drawing of Aaron by E. A. Abbey.)

T. M. Parrott: 'Shakespeare's Revision of "Titus Andronicus." ' In *Modern Language Review,* 1919, pp. 16-37. (An interesting discussion of the authorship of the play, presenting Shakespeare as the superficial reviser of an old play, and seeking to determine his share in *Titus* by metrical tests.)

H. Dugdale Sykes: *Sidelights on Shakespeare,* 1919. (Interesting and informative studies in the disputed plays of Shakespeare, concluding with the theory that Peele is the author of *Titus.*)

H. D. Gray: 'Shakespeare's Share in Titus Andronicus.' In *Philological Quarterly,* April, 1926, pp. 166-172. (The author applies the double-ending test to *Titus* to determine the share of Shakespeare in the play.)

J. M. Robertson: *An Introduction to the Study of the Shakespeare Canon,* 1924. (A revision of his earlier study, *Did Shakespeare Write 'Titus Andronicus'?* 1905. The most recent and most exhaustive study of the authorship of the play, in which the author discusses the conclusions set forth in most of the works listed above. Shakespeare's authorship of *Titus* is vigorously assailed, and the claims of other Elizabethans, especially those of Peele, to the authorship are set forth. The methods employed are those of the prosecuting attorney.)

Editions: Among the most useful are Knight's *Pictorial Shakespeare,* 1867, with a valuable 'Notice of the Authenticity of *Titus Andronicus*' (*Doubtful Plays,* pp. 46-59); the *Henry Irving Shakespeare,* 1890, Vol. VII, introduction by A. W. Verity, pp. 253-260; the *Bankside Shakespeare,* 1890, Vol. VII, introduction by Appleton Morgan; the *Cambridge Shakespeare,* by W. A. Wright, 1893, with full critical apparatus and exhaustive bibliography; and the *Arden Shakespeare,* 1904, edited by H. B. Baildon, with elaborate introduction and notes containing valuable illustrative material, not, however, always interpreted soundly.

INDEX OF WORDS GLOSSED

(Figures in full-faced type refer to page numbers)